"In this Scripture-satura
seling interactions and i.
training counselors to demonstrate how we can love, listen to, grieve
with, challenge, and accept the people around us in ways that befit the
gospel of the grace of Jesus."

Nancy Guthrie, Author of *Saints & Scoundrels in the Story of Jesus*

"Michael Emlet has written a very compassionate, biblical, and helpful
book, with practical guidelines for how to love others as God loves us.
It emphasizes the need to hold all three truths in a balanced perspective
for every person: as a saint in Christ, a sufferer, and a sinner. Highly
recommended!"

Siang-Yang Tan, Professor of Psychology, Fuller Theological
Seminary; author of *Shepherding God's People* and *Counseling and
Psychotherapy: A Christian Perspective*

"Dr. Michael Emlet has given us a treasure. He's primarily focused on
how we relate to others through the triple lens of saint, sufferer, and
sinner. He's particularly strong at blending those lenses together. The
result? You can begin to look at and treat people as fully human. His
experience as a counselor grounds his thoroughly biblical insights in
real life. This immensely helpful book isn't just for counselors—it's for
all of Jesus's followers."

Paul Miller, Author of *A Praying Life* and *J-Curve: Dying and Rising
with Jesus in Everyday Life*

"As Christians, we know we are called to love our neighbors as ourselves,
but it can be hard to know what it means to offer love to our neighbors
on the ground in concrete, daily ways. In this deep, rich, and practical
book, Michael Emlet draws on Scripture and years of experience as a
Christian husband, parent, church member, and counselor to help us
more faithfully and fully love our neighbors, our spouses, our children,
and all whom God brings into our lives. Through this exploration of
what it means that we are all simultaneously saints, sufferers, and sinners, which is shaped by the wisdom of the Bible on every page, those
who read this book will come away better equipped to fulfill the Great
Commandment in the quotidian moments of everyday life and ministry."

Kristen Deede Johnson, Dean and Professor of Theology
and Christian Formation, Western Theological Seminary;
award-winning author

"This book will give you a fuller view of yourself and those you love. It is clear, helpful, gentle, and wise, which just happens to be the way I would describe Mike."

Edward T. Welch, Faculty and counselor, Christian Counseling and Educational Foundation (CCEF); author of *A Small Book for the Anxious Heart*

"Every person who seeks counseling brings a unique blend of history, beliefs, behaviors, circumstances, and relationships, but there are fundamental truths that apply broadly to every person we minister to. Our identity before God as saints, sufferers, and sinners is perhaps *the* foundational truth upon which our counseling stands. *Saints, Sufferers, and Sinners* offers a deeply biblical and theological understanding of this reality and demonstrates how this broad principle fleshes out in the counseling experience with ground level practical application."

Curtis Solomon, Executive Director, The Biblical Counseling Coalition

"Two things I appreciate about Michael Emlet's new book: 1) its clarity regarding the realities of believers being saints, sufferers, and sinners while we walk this earth, and 2) its realistic application of our identity in Christ affecting each of these dimensions of our lives in the way that we live, love, counsel, encourage, correct, and repent for the sake of others."

Bryan Chapell, Pastor; author

"Too often we speak only to parts of people because we only see part of them: they just need to get over their sin, just need compassion because life has been hard, just need faith because it's all that matters. Mike Emlet's *Saints, Sufferers, and Sinners* refuses to over-simplify. Instead, Emlet enables his readers in concrete, biblically rich ways to simultaneously take all three aspects of our Christian, human reality seriously. Full of winsome case studies, this book brims with wisdom in action about gently responding to sin, practical ways to encourage, and how to offer meaningful comfort to those who suffer. *Saints, Sufferers, and Sinners* is the product of a lifetime of godliness from a man whose compassion and humble grace come through on every page. This must become a foundational book for biblical counselors of every type for generations to come."

J. Alasdair Groves, Executive Director, Christian Counseling and Educational Foundation (CCEF); coauthor of *Untangling Emotions*

"As a counselor, the value of seeing how the gospel speaks in unique ways to sin, suffering, and our identity as saints has been pivotal. As a pastor, these balanced truths are essential to being a good ambassador of the gospel. Michael Emlet's work in *Saints, Sufferers, and Sinners* is a must read for anyone wanting to accurately apply the gospel to the full breadth of human experience."

Brad Hambrick, Pastor of Counseling at The Summit Church; assistant professor of Biblical Counseling, Southeastern Baptist Theological Seminary; general editor for *Becoming a Church that Cares Well for the Abused*

"Many of us err in tending to see 'the problem' in ourselves or in others as only one of sin or idolatry, or entirely one of suffering, and in focusing on either we can forget that all God's people are also saints in whom the Spirit is at work already. *Saints, Sufferers, and Sinners* helps us see people as they really are. Where others stop, this accessible yet profound book also equips us for talking to those not yet safe in Christ's kingdom. This book is everyday practical, richly biblical, and wonderfully re-balancing."

Andrew Nicholls, Director of Pastoral Care, Oak Hill College, London

"With the precision of a physician and the compassion of a counselor, Michael Emlet offers readers a template for engagement and relationship that will help you reimagine gospel-centered counseling. Saturated in Scripture and brimming with real-life case studies, one can quickly recognize this is the fruit of many years of study in Scripture and walking with our Savior. Michael is the exact type of counselor I would want walking alongside me in my journey of faith."

Jonathan D. Holmes, Pastor of Counseling, Parkside Church; executive director, Fieldstone Counseling

SAINTS, SUFFERERS, AND SINNERS

LOVING OTHERS AS GOD LOVES US

Michael R. Emlet

New Growth Press

newgrowthpress.com

New Growth Press, Greensboro, NC 27401
newgrowthpress.com

Cover Design: Faceout Books, faceoutstudio.com
Interior Design and Typesetting: Gretchen Logterman

ISBN: 978-1-64507-051-1 (Print)
ISBN: 978-1-64507-053-5 (eBook)

Library of Congress Cataloging-in-Publication Data

Names: Emlet, Michael R., author.
Title: Saints, sufferers, and sinners : loving others as God loves us / Michael R. Emlet.
Description: Greensboro, NC : New Growth Press, [2021] I Series: Helping the helper I Includes bibliographical references. I Summary: "Counselor Michael R. Emlet outlines a model of one-another ministry based on how God sees his people as saints, while bringing comfort to the sufferer, and faithfully speaking truth to the sinner"-- Provided by publisher.
Identifiers: LCCN 2020038872 (print) I LCCN 2020038873 (ebook) I ISBN 9781645070511 (print) I ISBN 9781645070535 (ebook)
Subjects: LCSH: Love--Religious aspects--Christianity.
Classification: LCC BV4639 .E48 2021 (print) I LCC BV4639 (ebook) I DDC 259--dc23
LC record available at https://lccn.loc.gov/2020038872
LC ebook record available at https://lccn.loc.gov/2020038873

Printed in the United States of America

28 27 26 25 24 23 22 21   3 4 5 6 7

To Lydia and Luke,

You have reminded me of the love of my heavenly Father.
You have walked with me in sorrow and grief.
You have patiently borne my failures and sins, and freely offered me
forgiveness.

I am incredibly privileged to be your father.

CONTENTS

Part 1:
Understanding People

Chapter 1

OPERATING INSTRUCTIONS REQUIRED

Nearly everything we buy comes with instructions. Pieces of furniture come with assembly directions. Clothes come with laundering tips. Electronics come with operating instructions. And dozens of "how-to" books can help you learn any skill or trade. I tend to be rabid about seeking out instructions. I admit that sometimes I overdo it. My family still teases me mercilessly about the book I bought on how to raise a puppy, years before we actually had a dog. And then, once we got a dog, I never pulled it off the shelf. Sadly, our labradoodle Maddie is a poster dog for how *not* to raise a puppy! Operating instructions are clearly very important for navigating our world.

But don't you sometimes wish *people* came with operating instructions? Not that simple, right? Other people are complex. You and I are complex. How do we understand ourselves and each other? How do we move toward one another in

God-honoring ways? How do we love wisely in the context of everyday relationships and in more formal counseling settings?

LOVING WISELY IS NOT EASY

The practice of love takes many shapes in Scripture. We are commanded not to "wrong one another" (Leviticus 25:17). God calls us to sharpen one another as "iron sharpens iron" (Proverbs 27:17). We are to "show kindness and mercy to one another" (Zechariah 7:9) and "speak the truth to one another" (Zechariah 8:16). Jesus said, "Be at peace with one another" (Mark 9:50). The apostle Paul calls us to "love one another with brotherly affection," outdoing "one another in showing honor" (Romans 12:10). We are to "instruct one another" (Romans 15:14), "comfort one another" (2 Corinthians 13:11), and "bear one another's burdens" (Galatians 6:2). Paul urges us to address "one another in psalms and hymns and spiritual songs" (Ephesians 5:19). He tells us that we should be "teaching" and "admonishing" one another (Colossians 3:16). We are to "encourage one another and build one another up" (1 Thessalonians 5:11). James calls us to "confess your sins to one another and pray for one another" (James 5:16). That's a dizzying array of ways God calls us to move toward each other in love! Loving others in these multifaceted ways means that we need to know and understand people well. Love doesn't happen in abstraction but in concrete, person-specific ways.

But loving wisely and well is not easy, is it? Have you ever thought, "I don't really understand what's going on with this person; I don't know where to begin to help"? Or, "What I said made perfect sense to me, but she walked away from me in anger"? Do other people ever frustrate or mystify you? Do you zig in a relationship and afterwards realize that you should have zagged? You admonished when you should have comforted?

3

You brought consolation when speaking a challenging word would have been the better path of love? It's likely that you yourself been the recipient of misguided attempts to love. We struggle to love others well, and other people struggle to love us well.

A STRUCTURE TO HELP US UNDERSTAND EACH UNIQUE STORY

Each person's story is unique. Antonio seems to be a different person since returning from Iraq. He is distant from his wife and children and often explodes in rage at the slightest provocation. Carla is thirty-eight and longs to be a wife and mother. Now an engagement she broke off a decade earlier continues to haunt her. John and Sarah struggle to make ends meet financially with two children in college and a third child with chronic health problems. Olivia is a respected youth leader with a winsome knowledge of Scripture, yet she obsesses for hours each day about whether she truly is a child of God. Darren, a pastor in your church, just left his wife of twenty-eight years for his male lover, leaving behind a trail of devastated family members and congregants. These are the kinds of stories you will regularly hear if you are intent on loving others in the church. What stands out to you about each brief snippet of their stories? Is there anything that brings some unity amidst the diversity of their experiences?

While the specific shape and steps of ministry to these individuals should correspond to the particular realities and details of their experiences, Scripture gives us a kind of trellis—a basic structure—on which love can flower in person-specific ways. Though the Bible is not a technical operating manual like the detailed instructions that came with the unassembled bike you just bought, it does provide foundational categories that can help you understand others—and yourself—so that we might live wisely and fruitfully as his people (Psalm 119:105, 130; 2 Peter 1:3–4). That's what this whole book is about. In the next chapter, we will start by identifying three foundational and biblical ways of understanding your friends, family members, and counselees: saints, sufferers, and sinners.

Chapter 2

WHAT'S TRUE OF EVERY
BELIEVER YOU MEET?

What is true of yourself and every Christian you meet, according to Scripture? What can you be *sure* about your spouse, your roommate, your child, your friend—even a brother or sister in Christ who is at odds with you?

First, you can be sure that they *struggle with identity* at some level—which means they are implicitly or explicitly asking, "Who am I?" That is, "What is my core identity? How do I fundamentally conceive of myself? What do I highlight when I tell my story?" Because this identity question is tied to mission or calling, it also means they are asking, "What is my purpose? What should I be doing with my life? How should I be living in light of my basic identity? What difference does it make that I am a person in Christ?"

Second, you can be sure that they *struggle with evil*. This struggle with evil expresses itself in two ways. They experience evil from without (suffering), which means they are asking, "How do I deal with evil done to me? How should I persevere amidst the hardships and sorrows of my life?" They also experience evil from within (sin), which means they are asking, "How do I deal with the evil inside of me? How do I deal with the reality that 'when I want to do right, evil lies close at hand' (Romans 7:21)? Why do I struggle to live out of my identity? How do I change?"

You and I, and every Christian we meet, wrestle with these questions about identity and evil. This has been true ever since Adam and Eve deviated from God's original design for humanity. Thankfully, God brings a welcome sense of clarity to this complexity. Oliver Wendell Holmes is commonly attributed as having said, "I would not give a fig for the simplicity this side of complexity, but I would give my life for the simplicity on the other side of complexity." We all want truth that is simple and yet embraces the complex. Christians are blessed that God, in his Word, offers this to us. Scripture gives us basic—but not simplistic—categories for understanding our experiences as God's redeemed image bearers.

HOW DOES GOD MOVE TOWARD HIS PEOPLE?

These categories become apparent as we observe in the Bible how God moves toward people. At a most foundational level, the life, death, and resurrection of Jesus Christ restores our identity as children of the living God (1 John 3:1–2) and he overcomes evil, whether in the form of suffering (Matthew 4:23–24; Acts 10:38) or sin (Romans 3:23–24; 8:3–4; 2 Corinthians 5:21; Galatians 3:13). But the story of redemption is much more fine-grained than simply asserting and proclaiming these foundational truths. As we look closer, we see that Scripture models ministry to God's people in three distinct ways. This, in turn, helps us know how to move toward one another so that we're not just guessing or completely flying by the seat of our pants. So, what does Scripture show us?

Scripture reveals that God ministers to his people as:

- *Saints* who need confirmation of their identity as children of God,
- *Sufferers* who need comfort in the midst of their affliction, and
- *Sinners* who need challenge to their sin in light of God's redemptive mercies.[1]

Saint, sufferer, and sinner. All three of these are simultaneously true of every Christian you meet. If this is the way God sees and loves his people, then we should do the same, using these broad biblical categories to guide our overall approach to the people in our lives. They are signposts for wise love. They help you to prioritize one-another ministry, whether it's to your friend, husband, wife, roommate, child, coworker, or counselee.

WHAT ABOUT UNBELIEVERS?

These categories are true for every Christian, but what about unbelievers? Throughout this book, I'm going to focus primarily on relationships within the body of Christ, since I'm aiming this book toward helpers in the church. But let me offer an important aside on this question, because we all have family members and friends who are not Christians. Should we understand them the same way we understand other believers? Yes and no! Certainly, the most foundational biblical category that

---

1. See Michael R. Emlet, *CrossTalk: Where Life and Scripture Meet* (Greensboro, NC: New Growth Press, 2009), 74–79.

describes *all* people, both believers and unbelievers, is *God's image bearer* (Genesis 1:27; 5:1–2; Psalm 8:3–8). All people are created in the likeness of God, with its attendant moral, ethical, social-relational, and missional (vocational or ruling) aspects. As God's image bearers, we are his representatives, called to extend his good and wise rule over the earth (Genesis 1:28; 2:15). We work cooperatively in relationship as male and female image bearers to accomplish this noble task (Genesis 2:18). We are called to obey him (Genesis 2:16), as is befitting for the children of a holy God (Ephesians 4:24).

Sin distorts the image of God, but it does not erase it. Without Christ, we are totally depraved—sin affects every aspect of our personhood—but we are not as bad as we could be because of God's providence and common grace (Psalm 145:9; Matthew 5:45b; Hebrews 1:2–3). John Murray defines common grace as "every favor of whatever kind or degree, falling short of salvation, which this undeserving and sin-cursed world enjoys at the hand of God."[2] Each person you meet is a recipient of God's ongoing common grace, but only God's people can be identified as "saints"—sons and daughters of the living God. By contrast, here are some examples of how the unbeliever is described in the Scriptures:

- A slave/orphan (Galatians 4:1–7; Romans 8:14–15)
- Living in darkness instead of light (1 Peter 2:9–10)
- A slave of sin (Romans 6:17)
- Alienated and hostile in mind (Colossians 1:21)
- Far off (Ephesians 2:13)

Yet, despite these characteristics, the foundational category of "image bearer blessed by common grace" remains active in an

---

2. John Murray, "Common Grace," in *Collected Writings of John Murray*, vol. 2 (Edinburgh: Banner of Truth Trust, 1977), 96.

unbeliever. Because of this, Christians can approach them with eyes to see evidence of God's common grace in their lives, testify to God's saving grace made available through Jesus Christ, pray for God's kindnesses to lead them to repentance (Romans 2:4), and afford them the dignity that bespeaks an image bearer of the Creator of the universe.

Though unbelievers do not share in the identity of saint, the experiences of suffering and sin are common to both believers and unbelievers. In this way, we are more alike than different. Every person you meet has experienced bodily miseries, suffered at the hands of other people, or felt grief as a result of situational challenges and tragedies. And every person, believer or unbeliever, falls far short of even their own standards, let alone God's standards for holiness (Psalm 14:2–3; Romans 3:23). Sin is an ever-present reality.

Even here, however, there are distinctions to keep in mind. Although suffering is a tragic effect of the fall, it takes on a decidedly relational and redemptive significance for believers. Those who know Jesus are now yoked with him in their suffering (Philippians 3:8–11). They suffer in solidarity with Jesus Christ with the hope of the glory to come (2 Corinthians 4:16–18; 1 Peter 4:13–14). Similarly, although believers continue to struggle with sin in this life, their relationship to sin has been fundamentally altered due to the regenerating and sanctifying work of the Spirit (Titus 3:3–7). As the apostle Paul says, "How can we who died to sin still live in it?" (Romans 6:2). For believers, sin is an act of betrayal against their new identity. For unbelievers, sin is an act in keeping with their current identity (John 8:34; Galatians 5:19–21; Titus 3:3).

So, while the fundamental experiences of wrestling with one's identity, enduring bodily, relational, and situational suffering, and struggling with sin are universal problems, the specific contours of ministry will differ between believers and unbelievers as we employ the biblical categories of saint, sufferer, and sinner. Certainly, there is much commonality between believers and unbelievers in ministry approach, but I will also highlight differences to keep in mind as we move through the material.

For the remainder of this book, I will flesh out the categories of saint, sufferer, and sinner. My aim is for you to experience a greater clarity about how to love the people around you in wise, truthful, and compassionate ways. For each category, I will give an example of how Scripture models loving ministry to saints, sufferers, and sinners. And for each category I will give some practical examples of what that could look like in everyday relationships and in more formal ministry relationships. This doesn't mean that being mindful of the categories of saint, sufferer, and sinner will give you an exhaustive knowledge of the person before you. But these categories will help you press further into the relationship and prompt the kinds of questions and directions that will deepen your understanding of each unique person and give you specific ways to share the hope, comfort, and conviction of the gospel with those you are ministering to.

Chapter 3

JESUS CHRIST, THE ULTIMATE SAINT, SUFFERER, AND "SINNER"

Before traveling too far, it's important to connect our stories as saints, sufferers, and sinners with the story of Jesus Christ. Keeping Jesus central reminds us that these three categories are not abstract, but relational. We are saints, sufferers, and sinners in union with our Savior. He walked the path of humanity before us. He literally lived these experiences. He is the "founder and perfecter of our faith" (Hebrews 12:2). Through his life, death, resurrection, and ascension, Jesus fulfills each aspect of our human experience. So how does Scripture point to Jesus as the ultimate saint, sufferer, and "sinner"?

JESUS, THE ULTIMATE SAINT

First, Jesus embodies saintly identity as the Son of God, beloved of the Father. A declaration of his identity occurs at his baptism in Matthew 3. When he comes up from the water, the Spirit of

God descends on him and a voice from heaven says, "This is my beloved Son, with whom I am well pleased" (Matthew 3:17). Peter later confesses that Jesus is "the Christ, the Son of the living God" (Matthew 16:16). At the Transfiguration in Matthew 17:1–8, a voice from heaven declares, "This is my beloved Son, with whom I am well pleased" (17:5), an echo of the baptismal pronouncement. His identity as the Father's beloved Son is forever sealed in the resurrection. The apostle Paul notes that Jesus "was declared to be the Son of God in power according to the Spirit of holiness by his resurrection from the dead" (Romans 1:4).

This familial language is significant. In Luke's genealogy of Jesus, he ends with Adam, "the son of God" (Luke 3:38). He is not using "son of God" in an eternal divine sense, but in a relational, image-bearing sense. Paul describes Jesus as the second Adam, who perfectly fulfilled his role as the (human) son of God (Romans 5:12–21; 1 Corinthians 15:45, 47) as he, the eternal Son of God, became flesh (John 1:1, 14; Philippians 2:5–8). This was God's intent for humanity from the beginning, to be children bearing his likeness in his world for his glory. We were to have dominion over all creation (Genesis 1:28), serving as rulers in God's kingdom, which Graeme Goldsworthy describes as "God's people in God's place under God's rule."[1] Adam failed in this noble and kingly task. But God's design was not thwarted. From Adam's descendants, God chose Abraham and then the nation of Israel to bear his image and be a blessing to the world (Genesis 12:2–3). God repeatedly refers to the people of Israel as his child, son, or children (Exodus 4:22; Jeremiah 31:20; Hosea 11:1, 10; Malachi 1:6). He refers to himself as Israel's father (Jeremiah 31:9). King David and his descendants are also referred to with familial

---

1. Graeme Goldsworthy, *Gospel and Kingdom: A Christian Interpretation of the Old Testament* (Carlisle, UK: Paternoster Press, 1994), 46.

language (2 Samuel 7:14; Psalm 89:26–27), highlighting kingly or royal significance in bearing the identity of God's children.

Ultimately, Israel and even the line of King David could not faithfully live out their identity as God's children. Again and again, they rejected God as their father, choosing to follow other gods. As they turned away from their heavenly Father, they did not live in keeping with their identity. But Jesus is the obedient, faithful, loving son that Israel never was. He is the royal son, the King who ushers in his Father's kingdom. He perfectly lived out his Father's will and was vindicated by his resurrection from the dead (Romans 1:1–4). He now shares his place in God's family with brothers and sisters (see Hebrews 2:10–13, 17) by pouring out his Spirit, whom Paul calls "the Spirit of adoption" (Romans 8:15). Paul captures it this way in Galatians 4:4–7:

> But when the fullness of time had come, God sent forth his Son, born of woman, born under the law, to redeem those who were under the law, so that we might receive adoption as sons. And because you are sons, God has sent the Spirit of his Son into our hearts, crying, "Abba! Father!" So you are no longer a slave, but a son, and if a son, then an heir through God.

Jesus is the perfect saint/son. What does that mean for us? When we turn to Jesus in faith, his identity becomes our identity. We become, like him, God's favored child. In Christ, we are each an heir of the Father. Jesus the Son of God says, "I share my place in the royal family with you, fellow brother or sister. This is your new identity. Now you too can cry 'Abba, Father.'" For believers, being a "saint" is not a title but a mark of familial identity.

JESUS, THE SUFFERING SERVANT

Second, Jesus embodies the experience of a sufferer. He is *the* Suffering Servant (Isaiah 52:13–53:12). After his resurrection, on the road to Emmaus, Jesus helped Cleopas and another disciple see that his suffering and death was God's design throughout history. "'Was it not necessary that the Christ should suffer these things and enter into his glory?' And beginning with Moses and all the Prophets, he interpreted to them in all the Scriptures the things concerning himself" (Luke 24:26–27). Later Jesus appeared to a larger gathering, including the Eleven, and said, "Thus it is written, that the Christ should suffer and on the third day rise from the dead" (Luke 24:46).

We often think of Jesus's suffering in the context of his crucifixion and death. This is true, but in another sense, the whole of Jesus's life comprised suffering. Paul captures this in Philippians 2:5–8:

> Have this mind among yourselves, which is yours in Christ Jesus, who, though he was in the form of God, did not count equality with God a thing to be grasped, but emptied himself, by taking the form of a servant, being born in the likeness of men. And being found in human form, he humbled himself by becoming obedient to the point of death, even death on a cross.

Jesus suffered his entire life by setting aside his glory and rightful splendor. He faced the toils and trials every human being faces in a fallen world, all of the various evils "from without" that we experience, as I highlighted in our opening chapter. The writer of Hebrews describes him as the son who "learned obedience through what he suffered" (Hebrews 5:8). Earlier the writer said of Jesus, "For because he himself has suffered when tempted, he is able to help those who are being tempted" (Hebrews 2:18).

Jesus did not have, as we do, a sinful nature from which internal desires could arise that were at odds with his Father's will.[2] But he did face all the external pressures that we face—yet without turning away from his Father in heaven. We see one example of this in the record of Satan's frontal assault of Jesus in the wilderness after his baptism (Matthew 4:1–11 and Luke 4:1–13). Unlike Adam and Eve in the garden, Jesus did not succumb to the painful pressures of satanic testing.

Jesus is the archetypal sufferer. What does that mean for us? It means that when we experience suffering, we can turn to Jesus—a brother and a friend who understands suffering from the inside. It means we can pour out our troubles to one who is a man of sorrows and familiar with grief (Isaiah 53:3). Jesus the Suffering Servant says, "I know your pain and your agony. I have triumphed over suffering and death and I have given you my Spirit, the Comforter, to be with you. I stand ready to pour out grace and mercy in your time of need" (see Hebrews 4:15–16).

JESUS, THE SINLESS ONE WHO BECAME SIN

Third, Jesus is the sinless one who became sin. He is not a "sinner" in the way we are sinners, of course. Although he was "made like his brothers in every respect" (Hebrews 2:17), he did not participate in our sinful nature. The writer of Hebrews makes this clear when talking about Jesus as high priest of a better covenant:

---

2. See Ben Witherington III, *Letters and Homilies for Jewish Christians: A Socio-Rhetorical Commentary on Hebrews, James and Jude* (Downer's Grove, IL: IVP Academic, 2007), 160–61.

For it was indeed fitting that we should have such a high priest, holy, innocent, unstained, separated from sinners, and exalted above the heavens. He has no need, like those high priests, to offer sacrifices daily, first for his own sins and then for those of the people, since he did this once for all when he offered up himself. For the law appoints men in their weakness as high priests, but the word of the oath, which came later than the law, appoints a Son who has been made perfect forever. (Hebrews 7:26–28)

Paul describes the significance of Jesus, the sinless one, being condemned in our place this way: "For our sake he [God] made him [Jesus] to be sin who knew no sin, so that in him we might become the righteousness of God" (2 Corinthians 5:21; see also Romans 8:3–4). He became a curse for us so that through him we might receive the promised Holy Spirit (Galatians 3:13). He absorbed the full weight of human experience as sinner, having fully identified with us in our sinful condition.

In that sense, Jesus is counted as the archetypal sinner. What does that mean for us? Jesus—the Sinless One Who Became Sin—says, "I died to sin and rose again. I have given my Spirit to cleanse you from sin and to empower you to live in keeping with your new identity."

Taken together, our heavenly Father makes you part of his family by sending his Son into the misery of suffering and the crushing weight of sin so that his children ultimately may be free of this double curse. This means that regarding ourselves and others as saints, sufferers, and sinners puts us in the closest possible relationship to our Savior Jesus Christ.

Understanding ourselves and others as saints, sufferers, and sinners gives a biblical framework for personal ministry. Whether we are talking with a friend, giving pastoral advice, or counseling in a more formal setting, these categories can help us know where to start and give us a Scripture-based guide for our conversations. In the rest of the book, we will look at each aspect of saint, sufferer, and sinner more closely, applying these categories directly to our relationships and our counseling.

Part 2:
Loving Others as Saints

Chapter 4

SCRIPTURE SPEAKS TO SAINTS

Let me begin by mentioning something that is so obvious that we sometimes overlook it: Scripture is addressed to saints. The entire Bible speaks to God's people. It is God's revelation for his people, beginning with Israel and ending with the church. The very existence of God's Word presupposes the "saint" designation.[1] God does not reveal himself in the abstract to all people everywhere, but to a particular people, his chosen and beloved people, the descendants of Abraham, Isaac, and Jacob. And his word comes to Gentiles who have become part of Israel and thus members of God's family through the work of Jesus Christ (Romans 11). That Scripture is addressed to God's covenant people may be more obvious to us in the New Testament epistles, where Paul writes to different churches throughout the Mediterranean region, or when prophets in the Old Testament

---

1. This chapter is an expansion of material originally found in Michael R. Emlet, *CrossTalk: Where Life and Scripture Meet* (Greensboro, NC: New Growth Press, 2009), 75.

are calling upon Israel to repent. But each portion of Scripture, from Genesis to Revelation, has a particular occasion for its communication. God speaks not a generic word, but a specific and timely word to his beloved people at multiple points in redemptive history.

The great biblical theologian Geerhardus Vos said, "All that God disclosed of Himself has come in response to the practical religious needs of His people as these emerged in the course of history."[2] That's amazing! God tailors his communication to us, revealing what we need in a given moment. God knows his people need clarity about who he is and what he is doing in the world. He knows his people need clarity about their identity, their suffering, and their sin. And so, over the course of time, God acted redemptively and God spoke redemptively to frame his people's experience of life in a fallen world.

GOD'S PEOPLE ARE DEFINED BY THEIR RELATIONSHIP TO HIM

As God speaks to his beloved people, he frequently talks about their characteristics as his children. Throughout Scripture, he often explicitly reminds his people who they are in relation to him. Here are just a few of those reminders:

- We are image bearers of the one true and living God, called to exercise wise dominion over the earth (Genesis 1:26–28)
- We are those to whom and through whom the blessing of the nations has come (Genesis 12:2–3; Galatians 3:8–9)
- We are part of the community God chose and took for himself (Deuteronomy 4:32–40)

---

2. Geerhardus Vos, *Biblical Theology: Old and New Testaments* (Edinburgh: Banner of Truth Trust, 1975), 9.

- We are those who are distinguished by the very presence of God (Exodus 33:16; Romans 8:15)
- We are sanctified and justified in Christ Jesus (1 Corinthians 1:2; 6:11)
- We are chosen, redeemed, forgiven children of God in Christ, who have been given the Holy Spirit (Ephesians 1:3–14)
- We are adopted as God's children and named fellow heirs with Christ (Romans 8:15–17; Galatians 4:4–7)
- We are God's children now, but we are not yet fully what we will be, which is like Jesus himself (1 John 3:2)
- We are "a chosen race, a royal priesthood, a holy nation, a people for his own possession" (1 Peter 2:9)

Notice how closely connected the identity of God's people is to God himself. We are defined by our relationship with him and not by something inherent in ourselves. In a world that beckons people to define themselves by false and fading identities based on looks, intelligence, wealth, power, or accomplishments, this is good news. Unlike worldly sources and definitions of identity, our identity and inheritance in Christ never fades (1 Peter 1:3–4).

GOD'S PEOPLE NEED TO BE REMINDED OF THEIR IDENTITY

But we, and God's people before us, easily forget this amazing reality. In the midst of suffering and the temptations to sin, we are prone to identity amnesia. We forget who we are, and God needs to remind us again and again. In that sense, Scripture is an identity-forming communique from the Father to his children. While all Scripture is meant to provide a window of perspective on our standing as saints, I'll highlight a few places where God explicitly reminds his people who he is and what he has done for them.

When Moses encounters God in the burning bush, God self-identifies as "the God of your father, the God of Abraham, the God of Isaac, and the God of Jacob" (Exodus 3:6), which immediately puts Moses squarely in the middle of God's story of redemption. God instructs him to say to the Israelites, "I promise that I will bring you up out of the affliction of Egypt to the land of the Canaanites, . . . a land flowing with milk and honey" (Exodus 3:17), a promise originally made to Abraham hundreds of years earlier (Genesis 12:7; 17:8).

On the cusp of entering the promised land for the second time, Moses reminds those who have survived the wilderness experience who they are in relation to God:

> "For you are a people holy to the LORD your God. The LORD your God has chosen you to be a people for his treasured possession, out of all the peoples who are on the face of the earth. It was not because you were more in number than any other people that the LORD set his love on you and chose you, for you were the fewest of all peoples, but it is because the LORD loves you and is keeping the oath that he swore to your fathers, that the LORD has brought you out with a mighty hand and redeemed you from the house of slavery, from the hand of Pharaoh king of Egypt. Know therefore that the LORD your God is God, the faithful God who keeps covenant and steadfast love with those who love him and keep his commandments, to a thousand generations." (Deuteronomy 7:6–9)

This generation who heard Moses's words saw their parents die over a forty-year period as a result of the Exodus community's disobedience (Numbers 14:20–35; Joshua 5:6). Was God still with them? Were they still his chosen people? They needed reaffirmation of their identity as the very people of the one and only God.

At critical points in Israel's history, God reminds his people of his redemptive work and their position and calling as his children. Some examples of those occasions include the covenant renewal at the end of Joshua's life (Joshua 24), Samuel's farewell address (1 Samuel 12), God's covenant with David (2 Samuel 7), the dedication of the temple (1 Kings 8), and the covenant renewal among the returned exiles under Nehemiah (Nehemiah 9). Multiple psalms recount the history of Israel—78, 89, 105, 106, and 136—to name several. A repeated element in these passages is the retelling of the exodus story. It's no wonder that the exodus gets extended air time in the Old Testament: it represents an identity-forming moment in redemptive history, a work of God that ultimately points to Jesus's greater and final triumph over the powers of sin and death.

In the New Testament, the focus is on the life, death, and resurrection of Jesus Christ. Preaching pointed to Jesus's work as the fulfillment of God's promises to Abraham and the people of Israel (Acts 3:11–26; 7; 13). Jesus establishes a new covenant in his blood for God's people (Jew and Gentile alike), now anchoring their identity in him (Ephesians 2:11–21). Paul's repeated phrase "in Christ" shows just how intimately connected we are to Christ—our very selves are hidden with him (Colossians 3:4). Similar to what we see in the Old Testament, the New Testament writers remind their hearers of God's particular saving work in their lives, which is now fulfilled in Jesus

Christ (Philippians 1:6; Colossians 1:3–14; 1 Thessalonians 1:2–10; 2 Timothy 1:3–7).

Given that Scripture is addressed to God's people, the Bible is a powerful, identity-forming means of grace. Rehearsing the story of the gospel and our own personal connections to the story is an identity-shaping activity that we and others need daily. Every portion of Scripture invites us to live more fully in the reality of our adoption as sons and daughters of the living God.

It's a joy and a privilege to share this truth with others and see them be encouraged and transformed by remembering who they are in Christ. Right now I am meeting with a young Christian whose default view of himself is "worthless" and "incompetent." He often feels he is disappointing God and others, and that he must face life's challenges alone. He desperately needs a weighty counterbalance to these false narratives. It has been helpful for him to meditate at the start of each day on the reality that he is a son and not a slave/orphan (Galatians 4:7) and that he is not alone because of God's indwelling Spirit. And he is learning to recall with thankfulness the many ways his Father God pursued and rescued him in his darkest moments.

OUR IDENTITY AS SAINT IS FOUNDATIONAL

This brief story reminds us of one final and important point: for the believer, the designation "saint" is more foundational than the designation "sufferer" or "sinner." We experience a fundamental identity shift when we become believers. When we turn from our sin to God in repentance, receiving and resting on Jesus and his righteousness by faith, a seismic shift in our souls occurs. We are now people in Christ. Paul repeatedly highlights the nature of this profound transformation in his epistles:

- "So you also must consider yourselves dead to sin and alive to God in Christ Jesus" (Romans 6:11).
- "You are not your own, for you were bought with a price" (1 Corinthians 6:19b–20a).
- "I have been crucified with Christ. It is no longer I who live, but Christ who lives in me" (Galatians 2:20).
- "He has delivered us from the domain of darkness and transferred us to the kingdom of his beloved Son, in whom we have redemption, the forgiveness of sins" (Colossians 1:13–14) .
- "You turned to God from idols to serve the living and true God" (1 Thessalonians 1:9).

Ongoing struggle with suffering or with sin must be understood in this basic context of our new identity as children of the living God. We are saints who suffer. We are saints who sin. But we are saints nonetheless at our core.

So how do we love and minister to believers who may have forgotten, in the face of suffering and sin, their true standing and status before God? That is our focus for the next several chapters.

Chapter 5

HOW GOD LOVES SAINTS: A BIBLICAL EXAMPLE

Lee is a gifted musician and poet. He is well-liked and respected by the members of his small group, who see his heart to serve others and his desire to honor Christ through his music and writing. But he has struggled with overeating and pornography for many years. He wrestles deeply with shame and guilt over his failures. Sometimes he's hyper-focused on building a "streak of victorious days," only to experience profound disappointment and hopelessness when he sins. In those moments of failure, he wonders if God turns away in disgust. He finds it hard to imagine that God is at work in his life.

How do we encourage fellow believers like Lee in their identity as saints in Christ? Scripture itself models how to do this. In the preceding chapter I noted many places in the Bible that portray and establish the identity of God's people. Any of those passages would be fruitful to study in depth, but I'm going to focus on what we can learn from Paul's example in 1 Corinthians 1:1–9.

Paul, called by the will of God to be an apostle of Christ Jesus, and our brother Sosthenes, To the church of God that is in Corinth, to those sanctified in Christ Jesus, called to be saints together with all those who in every place call upon the name of our Lord Jesus Christ, both their Lord and ours: Grace to you and peace from God our Father and the Lord Jesus Christ. I give thanks to my God always for you because of the grace of God that was given you in Christ Jesus, that in every way you were enriched in him in all speech and all knowledge—even as the testimony about Christ was confirmed among you—so that you are not lacking in any gift, as you wait for the revealing of our Lord Jesus Christ, who will sustain you to the end, guiltless in the day of our Lord Jesus Christ. God is faithful, by whom you were called into the fellowship of his Son, Jesus Christ our Lord.

In his ministry to the Corinthians, Paul is intentional about highlighting various facets of Christian identity.

Let's look closely at the variety of identity statements Paul uses:

1. *The Corinthians are the "church of God"*—they are the gathered assembly of God called into existence by God himself. This means that identity is bestowed by God and has a communal aspect to it. It also means God's people are identified by his presence with them, and our identity is wrapped up in his presence with us. One of the most poignant examples of this in the Old Testament is when Moses is interceding on behalf of the Israelites soon after the golden calf incident. Moses says to God,

"If your presence will not go with me, do not bring us up from here. For how shall it be known that I have found favor in your sight, I and your people? Is it not in your going with us, so that we are distinct, I and your people, from every other people on the face of the earth?" And the LORD said to Moses, "This very thing that you have spoken I will do, for you have found favor in my sight, and I know you by name." (Exodus 33:15–17)

The reality that our identity is tied to God's presence is a key benefit for every Christian, and it is now guaranteed by the redemptive work of Jesus Christ. The gift, work, and presence of the Holy Spirit is synonymous with our new identity as children of God (Matthew 28:20; John 14:16, 25–26; Ephesians 1:13–14).

2. *The Corinthians are "those sanctified [that is, set apart, purified, and made perfect] in Christ Jesus."* Ordinarily when we speak of sanctification, we are referring to the ongoing process by which believers are gradually transformed into the character of Jesus Christ ("progressive" sanctification). But it's important to remember that there is a "definitive" (once-for-all) aspect to sanctification as well. John Murray notes, "What is most characteristic in definitive sanctification [is] death to sin by union with Christ in his death and newness of life by union with him in his resurrection."[1] This is especially seen in Romans 6:1–7:6. By the work of the triune God, there is a once-for-all definitive breach with sin that takes place at the inception of the Christian life. Our fundamental standing and identity is "perfect in Jesus Christ," even as we strive to live out that identity in ever-increasing conformity to his character. Hebrews 10:14 captures both the definitive and progressive aspects of our sanctification: "For by a single offering he has perfected for all time those who are being sanctified."

3. *Believers are "called to be saints" (his set apart and holy people).* "Saint" is the noun form of the same Greek root translated

---

1. John Murray, "The Agency in Definitive Sanctification," in *Collected Writings of John Murray*, vol. 2 (Edinburgh: Banner of Truth Trust, 1977), 285, footnote 2.

"sanctified" earlier in verse 2. "Sainthood" is not the designation for a small number of carefully vetted leaders throughout church history. Rather, "saint" was a title given to every Corinthian Christian as his or her basic identity. And this is true for all believers. Over eighty times throughout Scripture you see the term "saints" applied to God's people. This is especially true in the New Testament, but it can also be found in the Psalms and Daniel in the Old Testament. The apostle Peter highlights (and expands on) this aspect of our identity as Christians:

> But you are a chosen race, a royal priesthood, a holy nation, a people for his own possession, that you may proclaim the excellencies of him who called you out of darkness into his marvelous light. Once you were not a people, but now you are God's people; once you had not received mercy, but now you have received mercy. (1 Peter 2:9–10)

Peter also highlights that identity is tied with a calling: to "proclaim the excellencies of him who called you out of darkness." Identity is always tied to an ethical impulse, a way of living that is in agreement with one's identity.

4. *The Corinthians participate with "all those who in every place call upon the name of our Lord Jesus Christ."* They are part of a larger, worldwide community and movement, bigger than even the corporate gathering in Corinth. Are you staggered by that language? You should be! That's true of you too, as well as the believers you minister to. What an amazing foundation on which to build. What an amazing God and Father who gives us new identity in Jesus Christ, "to the praise of his glorious grace" (Ephesians 1:6).

Paul then highlights the ways he is thankful for the Corinthians, pointing out the evidences of God's grace he sees in their lives—in their speech, their knowledge, their gifts. He goes on to affirm the hope he has for their future: "You will be guiltless (or blameless) on the day of Christ Jesus. God has worked in your lives. He is working presently in your lives. And he will bring his work to completion" (author's paraphrase of 1 Corinthians 1:8–9). Paul says a similar thing in Philippians 1:6, "And I am sure of this, that he who began a good work in you will bring it to completion at the day of Jesus Christ."[2]

PAUL BEGINS WITH THEIR STATUS AS SAINTS

What is Paul's overall approach here? He deliberately begins with an affirmation of the Corinthians' standing in Christ and the good fruit he sees in their lives. He gives this affirmation knowing full well the sin issues he's going to address later in the letter—in fact, starting in the very next verse (10)! Some of the very things he praises the Corinthians for—their speech, their knowledge, their spiritual gifts—are the very things that are being abused in the church.

Clearly, Paul is not going to be soft on their sin—division, rivalry, sexual immorality, lack of love for the less wealthy members of the congregation, abuse of the Lord's supper, abuse of spiritual gifts, questions about the resurrection. These are not insignificant matters. And he *is* going to address these issues in his letter. Yet, look where Paul *begins*. He begins with the ministry priority of affirming and confirming their identity as saints in Christ. And except for the book of Galatians, that is what he does in all his epistles.[3]

I remember Tim Keller talking about this idea many years ago in a series of sermons he gave about marriage from Ephesians 5. He encouraged struggling couples to look for glimmers of their

---

2. See also 1 Thessalonians 5:23–24.
3. See Romans 1:1–15; 2 Corinthians 1:1–7; Ephesians 1:1–14; Philippians 1:1–11; Colossians 1:1–14; 1 Thessalonians 1:1–10; and 2 Thessalonians 1:1–4.

spouse's "glory self." That is, amidst the many things that irritate you, the places of hurt and sin, do you see the "self" that *is* currently in Christ, the "self" that he or she *will be* when Jesus returns? In a sense, it's having eyes to see what the apostle John says in 1 John 3:2, "Beloved, we are God's children now, and what we will be has not yet appeared; but we know that when he appears we shall be like him, because we shall see him as he is."[4]

Notice too this is not a form of spiritual flattery, as if we were saying, "I'm going to tell you what you want to hear to boost your self-confidence, but in reality, I think you're a jerk." No, Paul is highlighting what is really true about the Corinthians in Christ! Their very real and pressing problems don't change their fundamental identity. It's precisely because of his confidence in God's redemptive work in their lives that he can appeal to them to change in keeping with their true identity.

This gospel-generated confidence is exactly what Lee needed. As he grew to appreciate his fundamental identity as a saint united with Christ—"nothing can separate me from my merciful Savior!"—he turned more quickly to Jesus in the midst of his failures, rather than lingering in self-pity, self-condemnation, and shame. He became less concerned about keeping track of successes and more concerned with enjoying the presence of Jesus with him day to day. With the footing of his foundation more secure, Lee had the courage to talk about his struggles more openly with two men in his group. This led to a growing commitment to battle his sin patterns with their help and encouragement.

Now let's consider further how Paul's approach translates to our lives as helpers. What can we learn for our own ministry to others?

---

4. For further discussion, see Timothy Keller and Kathy Keller, *The Meaning of Marriage: Facing the Complexities of Commitment with the Wisdom of God* (New York: Dutton, 2011), 120–24.

Chapter 6

MINISTRY PRIORITIES FOR LOVING SAINTS

I talked recently with Christine, a woman who had suffered emotional and physical abuse, both in her family of origin and in her marriage, which ended in divorce. As we spoke, I learned that throughout her life, others had often pointed out the ways in which she was not measuring up. No one took seriously the possibility that she loved Jesus and wanted to serve him and others, despite her struggles. All they saw were her deficiencies, weaknesses, and sins. Her anger. Her disorganized house. Her fear of man. Her chronic tardiness. Her frequent absences at church. How would you enter into her life? What would catch your eye and shape your approach?

In the preceding chapter we noted Paul's approach to a church riddled with many such weaknesses and sins. What specific, one-another ministry priorities and implications flow from the example of Paul's approach to the Corinthians (and his approach in his other epistles)? That is, what should characterize our basic approach to our brothers and sisters in Christ, whether in formal or informal ministry settings? Here are ways you can follow Paul's approach to other saints in your midst:

- Be zealous to find evidences of God's grace in their lives.
- Eagerly point out where they demonstrate the character of Christ.
- Observe ways in which they are already living true to an identity in Christ and highlight them.
- Rather than embarking on an idol or sin hunt, first embark on a grace hunt.
- Highlight the good you see.
- Speak about how they have blessed and encouraged you as the aroma of Christ in your life (2 Corinthians 2:15).
- Notice where the Spirit is at work.
- Thank God for them in prayer.
- Communicate your love for them and God's love for them.
- Identify the gifts of the Spirit in their lives.
- Remind them of their destiny in Christ and the faithfulness of God in that journey.

Notice how positive and affirming this list is, and how aligned it is with the way Paul begins his letters to the saints, who comprise the various churches he loves.

ACTING AS A SIGNPOST FOR DISCOURAGED SAINTS

Approaching someone in these ways often does not come naturally. I'll discuss in a later chapter why we may find it difficult to encourage and highlight the good in others. That was certainly true of Christine's experience. What she got from others was constant critique, but what she needed the most was an identity advocate. She said to me, "I just needed someone to say, 'Fight! You can do it with God's help. You're his precious daughter!'" She needed someone who celebrated with her Christ's work on her behalf. Someone to observe the ways she engaged the broken and marginalized in her community. Someone to notice her small steps of obedience.

This doesn't mean you sugarcoat or overlook shortcomings and wrongdoings. It's an issue of ministry priority—what does this person most need to hear right now? I find that many people, particularly those who are discouraged, anxious, and depressed, have trouble noting the good that God has been up to in their lives. In that sense, I am acting as a signpost for them that points out, "You are a beloved saint and I see God's grace *here*!"

One of the people who does this consistently in my life is my former pastor, Joe Novenson. We joke that he must have given several assistants carpal tunnel syndrome over the years due to the hundreds of letters he dictates annually to current and former parishioners and friends. Although we are now geographically distant, he will write to my wife and me several times a year, encouraging us in our struggles and highlighting how he is praying for us and our children. (This is on top of his usual practice of following up each pastoral visit in his current church with a letter!) His most recent letter arrived two weeks ago and said simply,

> I wanted this letter to arrive at work so it might be a small encouragement to you, Mike. It is before sunrise and I am praying for you. I lift you before God's throne and I lift Lydia and Luke and Jody. May God show you the strength of His hand and His gentle keeping grace, even before the sun sets today. Ever know that it is a

privilege to be near you. You are loved and respected in ways that only heaven will let you know.

Enclosed with the letter was a selection from Spurgeon's *Treasury of David*, on "liquid prayers"—how God hears the voice of our weeping when words may fail us. Joe's letter served as a blessing that day, encouraging me to continue to live out who I really am—a son of our heavenly Father.

The first question of the Heidelberg Catechism is, "What is your only comfort in life and in death?" The answer begins, "That I am not my own, but belong, body and soul, in life and in death, to my faithful Savior Jesus Christ."[1] This is an identity statement, first and foremost. What is most true about me is not that I'm husband to Jody and father to Lydia and Luke. Or that I'm a faculty member at CCEF. Or that I tend to be a logical thinker. Or that I have some artistic skills. Or that I tend toward a melancholic disposition. Or that I face an array of particular hardships. Or that I struggle with particular sins. No doubt these things are true and contribute in important ways to who I am and how I am known by others. But what is most important about me—and about you and the person next to you in the pew—is that we are saints, children of the living God, who belong body and soul to him. That's our starting point in our relationships with believers.

---

1. Christian Reformed Church, *Ecumenical Creeds and Reformed Confessions* (Grand Rapids, MI: CRC Publications, 1988), 13.

Chapter 7

HOW WE LOVE SAINTS: EVERYDAY EXAMPLES

Encouraging Christians with what is praiseworthy in their lives might sound good in theory, but how does it work in practice? Let's consider some everyday examples starting with how loving others as saints looks like in parenting. How should I minister to my children as beloved sons and daughters?

For starters, here's how *not* to do it! Several years ago, both of my teenaged children were home for the day by themselves. When I returned from work, what caught my attention right away was the absence of the living room curtains. (Backstory— my children have voiced their disapproval of our lacy curtains). My son was sitting in the living room playing a computer game as I started the inquisition: "Why are the curtains down?" He answered, "Lydia washed them." (I'm thinking, *Shouldn't they be dry-cleaned rather than washed?*) "Why didn't you call and ask for permission?" You can see the parenting failures multiplying! First, my son wasn't the person to direct my questions to, my daughter was. Second, my tone was accusatory and irritated. I walked out of the room into our kitchen and after a few moments of silence, my son said, "Dad, did you notice how Lydia cleaned and organized everything?" Amidst all that good, which I had barely seen out of the corner of my eye, I had focused on the one thing that bothered me—and it wasn't even that important. It wasn't even a sin issue.

Here's the lesson: While, of course, it is important to address sins in my children's lives, do I notice them doing something good and praiseworthy? And do I let them know I see it? Even more importantly, do I communicate frequently, "You are my beloved son/daughter with whom I am well pleased"? Or "You are God's beloved child"? Baseline. Period. Without qualification.

A BENEDICTORY STANCE TOWARD OTHERS

Several months ago, at the men's retreat for our church, the speaker focused on the qualities of love found in 1 Corinthians 13:4–7. He described love as a "benedictory stance toward others."[1] A benediction literally means "good speaking." Our retreat speaker called it a posture that declares, "I am thankful that you *are*," a glad affirmation simply that you exist in the world and that you are in my life. Too often, our affirmation of others is tied to their performance, but the benedictory stance characteristic of love simply focuses on people as beloved image bearers of God. Remember Deuteronomy 7:6–9, where God reminds his people that they are his treasured possession? We too want to communicate to our brothers and sisters in Christ, "You are treasured." God did not choose Abraham based on his merits. And Israel certainly didn't deserve God's love after their

1. Sam Wheatley, unpublished teaching, March 22, 2019.

multiple failures in the wilderness. God simply chose them as the recipient of his covenantal love. "I love you because I love you," is the answer to the Christian's question, "Why do you love me, God?" When a pastor pronounces a benediction at the end of worship, it is a blessing from God himself, communicating that we go out into the world under the banner of his love.[2]

This happened at Jesus's own baptism. The affirmation from God the Father came at the start of his formal ministry. The declaration was not, "You've done well these first thirty years, let's see how the next three turn out." Rather, God said, "This is my beloved Son, with whom I am well pleased" (Matthew 3:17; see also Luke 3:22). The Father loves the Son from all eternity. Baseline. Period. Without qualification. This declaration is now over the lives of all those who are in Christ. His banner over each of us reads, "This is my beloved child, with whom I am well pleased."

While this particular moment was unique to Jesus, we will have many informal opportunities to bring encouragement (a benedictory stance) to our spouses, children, friends, and small group members. Remember, as C. S. Lewis said in *The Weight of Glory*, "There are no *ordinary* people. You have never talked to a mere mortal."[3] We were made for glory. To borrow phrasing from Lewis, how do you help someone toward that destination? I've looked at parenting, but consider how ministry priorities for saints could look in other relationships and situations.

---

2. One of the more familiar benedictions in Scripture is the Aaronic blessing found in Numbers 6:24–26, "The Lord bless you and keep you; the Lord make his face to shine upon you and be gracious to you; the Lord lift up his countenance upon you and give you peace."

3. C. S. Lewis, "The Weight of Glory" in *The Weight of Glory and Other Essays* (New York: Touchstone/Simon & Schuster, 1996), 39.

ENCOURAGING YOUR SPOUSE

Marriage is a perfect place to practice this encouragement. It's very easy, particularly after being married for several years, to get into relational ruts and take the other person for granted. Life, particularly if children are in the mix, can become about juggling work and school schedules, tag-team parenting, house and yard maintenance, meal prep, and cleaning. But we want more than a "divide and conquer" partnership in marriage. We want to encourage each other's growth in the Lord. We want to notice glimpses of glory in the other. In the midst of your daily routine, do you see where the Spirit is at work in your spouse? I know I can be more proactive here. I recently said to my wife Jody, after hearing her desire to bless a struggling friend, "You are a genuinely kindhearted and merciful person. I love that about you." I'm sure this was not news to her after twenty-two years of marriage, but it meant a lot to her that I observed this fruit of God's Spirit in her life. I also tell her how amazed I am by her perseverance and godly attitude in the midst of serious and chronic health problems. Faced with what she endures each day, I suspect I would curl up in a fetal position and not leave the bed! But she presses on, in love for God and for others. That is a praiseworthy work of God in her life to speak aloud.

Noticing the good in your spouse is particularly important if a pattern of bickering and negativity is characteristic of your marriage.[4] While working through underlying specific issues and relational dynamics is critical and often time-consuming, one simple practice that can help arrest a fall down the slope toward further anger and bitterness is to self-consciously look for the places where, amidst the day-to-day difficult interactions, you catch a whiff of the aroma of Christ, and you speak it out loud to

---

4. I am not speaking here about abusive marriages, which require particular forms of skilled pastoral care and intervention.

your spouse. "A soft answer turns away wrath" (Proverbs 15:1a). This is difficult, no doubt, and doesn't minimize sin issues that require careful attention, but it communicates, "You are more than the worst I often see in you." In a believer, there is always something redemptive to notice and to celebrate.

ENCOURAGING THE SAINTS IN YOUR CHURCH

How might this posture of confirmation or encouragement in Christ look in the life of the local church? I'll mention two places in particular. Are there people you avoid at church simply because you find them difficult to relate to because of their eccentricities or their interpersonal style? Perhaps you find them overly talkative, consistently self-absorbed, or often displaying a negative, critical spirit. A commitment to love the saints means you embrace the mind-set Paul describes in 1 Corinthians 12:21–22, "The eye cannot say to the hand, 'I have no need of you,' nor again the head to the feet, 'I have no need of you.' On the contrary, the parts of the body that seem to be weaker are indispensable." Approaching the person in your congregation that you tend to avoid communicates, "We are fellow heirs, together with Jesus Christ. I want to treat you as a beloved and indispensable brother or sister." Do you see how such a mind-set might revolutionize life together?

Here's another place of application in your church. Consider how a commitment to encourage a person in Christ might look in your small group Bible study. You've just asked a question and perhaps the person who responds is clearly off-base (but not heretical!) in his answer. Affirm what is admirable about the response before offering any gentle correctives.

We've seen how a commitment to love the saints well might look in everyday informal relationships such as parenting, marriage, and within the body of Christ. We will spend the next chapter unpacking how it might look in a more formal counseling relationship.

Chapter 8

HOW WE LOVE SAINTS: COUNSELING EXAMPLES

The very fact that someone seeks counseling generally means they are facing a challenging or intractable difficulty. By definition, there is a problem focus involved in counseling ministry. Everything is *not* good. Suffering and sin cloud perspective. Help is needed.

Counseling is hard work. It involves a deep dive into the particulars of suffering and sin in the context of a trusting relationship. In the midst of talking about all that is not right, it's important to surface for air and gain fresh gospel perspective. Sometimes all the person (and the counselor!) can see are the problems at hand. Because of this, I make it a priority in every session to highlight some evidence of God's grace I see in my counselees' lives. They need that encouragement just as much as you and I need that regular encouragement.

LOOK FOR THE WORK OF THE SPIRIT IN COUNSELEES

Let me give a few examples of what this looks like in counseling. I met with a young couple who were convinced their marriage was in terrible shape because they struggled to change fear-based patterns of communication that resulted in smoldering conflict for several days at a time. As I got to know them and their heart for Jesus, and as I observed the honest, constructive conversation between them, I highlighted the work of the Spirit in their lives. They were committed to honoring Jesus. They were committed to honoring the one flesh covenant they had made in marriage. Further, the level of vulnerable communication I saw between them put them miles ahead of many other couples I had counseled. They found that perspective hopeful. In the midst of their very real struggles, all they could see were their difficulties. As a result, they concluded that no other couples around them could be doing as poorly as they were. There certainly was work to do to improve their relationship, but they no longer felt like "outliers" as they fought for their marriage.

Here's another example. I counseled a man who struggled with anxiety and alcohol misuse. Much of his anxiety was related to people-pleasing, over-responsibility, and the pressure of performing well in social settings. He would drink in the evenings to calm himself and to disconnect from his fears. Over time, he gained a better sense of how to steward his time to honor the Lord, including the wisdom of learning how to say "no" in gracious ways to requests that were not related to areas of ultimate responsibility, whether at work or at home. He gained confidence in social settings and was increasingly motivated to love others well, rather than perform so that he looked good. His anxiety was much less overall. But he continued to wrestle with his alcohol use, which made him feel as though no progress had been made. It was helpful for him to take a step back from the "microscopic" day-by-day view, and instead observe the broader "landscape" of his life over the course of many months, noticing the many places where God had worked in his life. These critical changes at the heart level of his desires, fears, and motivations were important precursors to improvement in his drinking patterns, which we both longed to see change over time.

USE GOD'S WORDS TO ENCOURAGE COUNSELEES

Often as I work with counselees, I will use specific texts from Scripture to explicitly address them as saints and encourage them in what I see that is praiseworthy in their lives. I find that slowing down to look at a particular passage may have more "staying power" in a counselee's life than a passing encouragement on my part, as earnest as it may be. While I want my words of encouragement to be in line with Scripture, there's no substitute for actually interacting with a specific passage. I'll give two examples.

Jeff is a thirty-eight-year-old assistant pastor who recently resigned from his position when it became clear that years of conversation regarding the autocratic leadership style and decision-making approach of the senior pastor had not resulted in change. While he was not actually forced to resign, he certainly was pressured to do so because of his reluctance to implement changes in his approach to congregational care that he believed were unwise. He felt his only option was to leave.

What is hardest, however, is that the congregation, who loves him dearly, is confused about his departure. From their perspective, everything was going well. And Jeff, in his desire to avoid slander and gossip, has not talked to congregants about the tensions over the years. The elders know, and several are sympathetic to Jeff. But this is not public. At the same time, the leadership has spun Jeff's departure as "God's calling to new ministry ventures." In the midst of this, Jeff has experienced anger and bitterness. He is troubled greatly by his feelings, and we have talked about how to take his distress to the Lord using psalms of lament. But he is worried that once he leaves in a few months, he will become increasingly embittered by the injustices he and his family have faced. What passage would you use to encourage him? During one recent session, I took him to Galatians 6:7–9:

> Do not be deceived: God is not mocked, for whatever one sows, that will he also reap. For the one who sows to his own flesh will from the flesh reap corruption, but the one who sows to the Spirit will from the Spirit reap eternal life. And let us not grow weary of doing good, for in due season we will reap, if we do not give up.

Why did I use this passage? I wanted him to see how he was sowing seeds daily to guard against long-term bitterness. He struggled with anger, yes, but he also exhibited godly lament, grief, gratitude, and the practice of thanksgiving. At baseline, Jeff had a soft heart. I wanted to encourage him not to become weary in well-doing, for I already saw how it was bearing fruit in his life. It's true that this particular passage cuts both ways, and I have used it as a warning in other counselees' lives. But for Jeff, I wanted to underscore how I saw him sowing to please the Spirit. Let's move to a second example.

Kyle is a twenty-eight-year-old man who has struggled with narcotic abuse in the past and alcohol abuse in the present. Over the last six months he has remained sober. But not just sober in terms of abstinence. Rather, what I have seen in him is a growing "sober-mindedness" about his life and his calling as a husband and father (1 Peter 1:13). Rather than withdrawing into himself and seeking escape when he becomes anxious about the responsibilities of life, he increasingly moves toward his wife to share what's on his heart and mind, which has led them to pray together more frequently. He has also been more attentive to the needs of his wife and young son, pressing in to build his relationships with them and leaning against his tendency toward seeking comfort and ease. Just as importantly, he has become more involved in his local church, and he has built honest relationships with several elders who are familiar with his struggles. He is not allowing shame and fear of man to stand in the way of relationships with these men, all of whom he greatly esteems.

Again, I could have simply identified this constellation of changes as God's work in his life, and that would have been helpful. But I also wanted to paint a biblical vision for persevering in these changes. So, what passage would you choose? 1 Thessalonians 4:1, 9–10 came to my mind:

> Finally, then, brothers, we ask and urge you in the Lord Jesus, that as you received from us how you ought to walk and to please God, just as you are doing, that you do so more and more. . . . Now concerning brotherly love you have no need for anyone to write to you, for you yourselves have been taught by God to love one another, for that indeed is what you are doing to all the brothers throughout Macedonia. But we urge you, brothers, to do this more and more.

I wanted to highlight that he was living consistently in the way of love. Not only was he abstaining from alcohol, but he was also actively engaging the people in his life. Given that pattern of sanctification, what would further growth look like? To do so more and more. And with that, we started talking about what it would look like for him to transition out of regular counseling.

HOW DOES THIS LOOK WITH UNBELIEVERS?

As I mentioned earlier, we cannot appeal to the identity of "saint" for those who do not know Jesus. But we share the experience of living in God's world as God's image bearers and as recipients of his common grace. I believe this is why Paul began his ministry in Athens as he did, by highlighting evidence of the Athenian's inclination to worship, which is a hallmark of an image bearer.

> So Paul, standing in the midst of the Areopagus, said: "Men of Athens, I perceive that in every way you are very religious. For as I passed along and observed the objects of your worship, I found also an altar with this inscription: 'To the unknown god.' What therefore you worship as unknown, this I proclaim to you. The God who made the world and everything in it, being Lord of heaven and earth, does not live in temples made by man, nor is he served by human hands, as though he needed anything, since he himself gives to all mankind life and breath and everything. And he made from one man every nation of mankind to live on all the face of the earth, having determined allotted periods and the boundaries of their dwelling place, that they should seek God, and perhaps feel their way toward him and find him. Yet he is actually not far from each one of us, for 'In him we live and move and have our being';

as even some of your own poets have said, 'For we are indeed his offspring.'" (Acts 17:22–28)

Paul went on to proclaim their need to turn to Jesus, whom God raised from the dead. But take note of where he began. He highlighted their idolatry as evidence of hearts that are restless until they find their rest in the true God (to paraphrase Augustine). He springboards from evidences of common grace and the image of God to a call to embrace redemptive grace. He encouraged them that they were on the right track in some way, even while they were missing the true God who was calling out to them. While some of Paul's hearers mocked him, others wanted to learn more, and some became believers.

How might this happen in counseling ministry? Several years ago, I counseled a man who was referred to me by his Christian employer for help with an anger problem. While he did not profess faith in Christ, he was open to receiving biblically-based counsel. I was glad for his willingness to seek help, especially from a Christ-centered perspective. I highlighted his motivation to change. I affirmed his growing realization that his anger was creating distance in his closest relationships. I celebrated his deep concern and love for his girlfriend, who struggled with a chronic medical condition. From there we talked about his fears and desires that manifested as control and anger in his relationships and at his workplace. We framed his fears and desires as signposts pointing to God, markers of the fact that he was indeed built to be a worshiper—either of God or of created things (Romans 1:18–32).

Ultimately, we spoke about the need to embrace the call of Jesus as the means to true and lasting change, which he was not ready to do. But my first words to him were *not*, "I'm sorry, I can't help you until you profess faith in Jesus. Otherwise, we'll just be rearranging the deck chairs on the *Titanic*." Rather, I started with encouragements in the context of God's common grace to him. So, although he was not a saint in whom I could confirm his identity in Christ, I could employ the same ministry priority of noticing the good that God had already graciously worked in his life, while at the same time pointing him to the One who is the way, the truth, and the life (John 14:6).

Chapter 9

BARRIERS TO LOVING OTHERS AS SAINTS

As a counseling intern at the Christian Counseling & Educational Foundation (CCEF), I regularly presented new cases to my supervisor, Ed Welch. He routinely asked a question regarding my experience of my counselee, which at first was a bit puzzling: "Do you like him (or her)?" *Like him?* What does that have to do with anything? But Ed was probing my heart. His deceptively simple question forced me to reckon with deeper questions such as, "Do you find it easy to move toward this person? Do you see the good in his life? Are you glad God brought this person into your life?" In effect he was asking, "Is it easy or difficult for you to love this brother or sister?" The fact is, in both informal and formal helping relationships, loving others as saints is challenging.

Why might we struggle to love others as saints? Usually it's because of our own issues and blind spots. I'll identify seven reasons why confirming someone's Christian identity in encouraging and specific ways may be challenging for us as friends and helpers.

1. We ourselves are not living out our identity as those who have experienced the grace, mercy, and forgiveness of Jesus Christ, so we fail to notice it in others as well. Jesus highlighted this problem when he was at the home of Simon the Pharisee, who was appalled by the presence of a "sinner," a woman who anointed and kissed Jesus's feet while he reclined at the table. All Simon could see was her sinful manner of life. He judged both the woman and Jesus. In his eyes, she was neither saint nor sufferer, but only sinner. That was her unchangeable identity. Through a parable, Jesus rebuked the Pharisee, contrasting his grudging hospitality with the lavish love of the woman, a sign that she understood both her great sin and also her great forgiveness in Jesus (Luke 7:36–50). We can be a lot like Simon, not understanding or acknowledging our own deep need for a Savior. Stingy, judgmental hearts are reluctant to praise others. But when we realize the extent of the debt that God cancelled for us in Christ Jesus, we will humbly celebrate that work in others' lives as well.

2. We have tendencies toward performance and perfectionism. People like that are hard on themselves and they are hard on others. Such a mind-set makes us trigger-happy to identify and root out sin—those places where we and others miss the mark. I wonder if this reversion to a law mind-set rather than a cross-centered one is what led the Galatians to bite and devour one another (Galatians 5:15)? If you functionally live as though your standing before God is ultimately secured by what you do rather than what you've been given, it will be easier to notice what's wrong with others rather than God's gracious work in their lives.

3. We are not grateful. This is a corollary to my first point. If we don't recognize and thank God for his many gifts to us each day (the chief of which is Christ himself), we will have trouble seeing the evidences of God's grace in other people's lives. If we

are shortsighted when it comes to recognizing our Father's gracious handiwork in our own lives, we will miss those signposts of sainthood in others. Becoming more skilled in recognizing the work of the Spirit in our lives helps us notice and celebrate his good work in others' lives.

4. We are afraid that if we highlight the good we see in someone's life, we will confirm that nothing really needs to change in his or her life, despite obvious issues of sin being present. We may fear that people will hear our praise as an excuse for their self-justifying, blame-shifting, and victim mentality. While these may sometimes be valid fears, this mind-set misses the active and ongoing work of the Spirit in a believer's life, especially when it's hard to discern. (However, there *are* times when it is unwise to begin with the good—the next chapter will go into greater detail about those exceptions.)

5. We underestimate the role of positive feedback in our own growth as Christians, despite having experienced (hopefully!) the benefit of someone else's encouragement. The business world has noted this tendency as well. Employers think that giving corrective feedback (what needs to change) is more important than positive feedback for a job well done. "They vastly underestimate the power and necessity of positive reinforcement. Conversely, they greatly overestimate the value and benefit of negative or corrective feedback."[1] If giving positive feedback makes managers more effective, surely we, who have all the riches of God's grace, become more effective helpers when we model God's priority of reminding his people of their standing in Christ and the good fruit that grows from being united to him.

---

1. Jack Zenger and Joseph Folkman, "Why Do So Many Managers Avoid Giving Praise?" *Harvard Business Review*, May 2, 2017, https://hbr.org/2017/05/why-do-so-many-managers-avoid-giving-praise.

6. We can be passive and self-absorbed relationally. It takes thought and relational attentiveness to proactively be on the lookout for the Spirit's movement in a person's life and then to speak of it in specific ways. It's easier just to stay silent.

7. Personality and gifting also play a role. Some helpers are more naturally inclined to be mercy-oriented encouragers, whereas other helpers are more inclined to speak directly and forthrightly about concerns they have. Which are you? Neither leaning is better than the other. It's important to be aware of your tendencies and to ask God to stretch and grow you. Celebrating the good you see in someone's life *and* being honest about problems you observe are both essential because they keep God in the picture. But as you minister to believers, never forget that their baseline identity in Christ means that you expect to see the fruit of the Spirit in their lives.

Given these barriers, it's not surprising that there is indeed an art to loving saints well. With certain exceptions (described in the next chapter), this should be our starting place in ministry to others. In this way, we model how God himself approaches his people. Of course, we should not cry, "'Peace, peace,' when there is no peace" (Jeremiah 6:14), but we must be careful not to have eyes *only* for sin, and miss the marks of God's gracious work in his people's lives.

Chapter 10

WHEN NOT TO START WITH THE GOOD

I had just met Glen for the first time. As he spoke of his long-standing history of bipolar disorder, he casually mentioned that he had put the barrel of a loaded gun in his mouth earlier in the day. He had no hope and could give no reasons for living. He wasn't sure why he didn't pull the trigger, and he couldn't give any guarantee that he wouldn't end his life after our appointment.

Are there exceptions to the general rule of starting with the good you notice in someone's life? Yes. You just read of one such instance. One possible exception is when the suffering and sin patterns in your friends or counselees are especially dangerous, either to themselves or to others. Paul's letter to the Galatians is a clear example of this exception.[1] Without any commendation of the good, he launches into his concerns:

---

1. See also the messages to the churches in Sardis (Revelation 3:1–6) and Laodicea (Revelation 3:14–22). In both cases Jesus begins by pointing out issues of sin before highlighting the good (at least in Sardis; no commendation is given to the church in Laodicea.)

I am astonished that you are so quickly deserting him who called you in the grace of Christ and are turning to a different gospel—not that there is another one, but there are some who trouble you and want to distort the gospel of Christ. But even if we or an angel from heaven should preach to you a gospel contrary to the one we preached to you, let him be accursed. (Galatians 1:6–8)

This language is strong, but remember that Paul is building on a pre-existing relationship with the Galatians. Although he begins the substance of his letter with a clear call-out of their sin, it is done in the context of already knowing and caring for them. Further, Paul's greeting establishes his basic conviction of their standing in Christ when he says, "To the churches of Galatia: Grace to you and peace from God our Father and the Lord Jesus Christ, who gave himself for our sins to deliver us from the present evil age, according to the will of our God and Father, to whom be the glory forever and ever. Amen" (Galatians 1:2b–5). Having this conviction is what makes him all the bolder. "What then has become of all your blessedness?" he says later (Galatians 4:15). He's seen their joy and freedom up close and personal! This is not a detached, "holier than thou" denunciation of sin, but a bold, loving entreaty to deal with sin patterns that are threatening the very foundations of the gospel—and threatening to destroy the faith and well-being of God's people. Even when a stern rebuke is the ministry priority, the goal is rescue with the motive of love.

WHEN WE SHOULD *NOT* BEGIN WITH ENCOURAGEMENT

What might be some of the closest modern-day equivalents to this? When should we *not* take time to encourage first? One situation in which we should *not* spend time looking for the good is when we see an urgent and serious problem such as abuse (of children, of the elderly, or in marriages). God's most pointed words are directed toward those in authority who have oppressed and harmed the least among us. Let's look at a few places in Scripture where we see this.

In Jeremiah 23, God says,

> "Woe to the shepherds who destroy and scatter the sheep of my pasture!" declares the Lord. Therefore thus says the Lord, the God of Israel, concerning the shepherds who care for my people: "You have scattered my flock and have driven them away, and you have not attended to them. Behold, I will attend to you for your evil deeds," declares the Lord. "Then I will gather the remnant of my flock out of all the countries where I have driven them, and I will bring them back to their fold, and they shall be fruitful and multiply. I will set shepherds over them who will care for them, and they shall fear no more, nor be dismayed, neither shall any be missing," declares the Lord. (Jeremiah 23:1–4)

And in Ezekiel 34 the indictment is even more stern:

> "You eat the fat, you clothe yourselves with the wool, you slaughter the fat ones, but you do not feed the sheep. The weak you have not strengthened, the sick you have not healed, the injured you have not bound up, the strayed you have not brought back, the lost you have not sought, and with force and harshness you have ruled them." (Ezekiel 34:3–4)

In the New Testament, Jesus rebukes the religious leaders for the multiple ways in which they mistreat and mislead the people: "They tie up heavy burdens, hard to bear, and lay them on people's shoulders, but they themselves are not willing to move them with their finger" (Matthew 23:4). And Jesus further says to these religious leaders, "you shut the kingdom of heaven in people's faces. For you neither enter yourselves nor allow those who would enter to go in" (Matthew 23:13).

These are life-and-death matters. It's not that God's prophets or Jesus views oppressors or self-oriented leaders in a subhuman way, as if that gives license for stinging rebuke. Rather, what takes precedence is protecting others from harm by calling out the evil perpetrated by the oppressor. One image bearer is harming another image bearer. When we encounter such oppression, we must act to protect victims and call perpetrators to account. Often this entails the involvement of law enforcement personnel and child/elder protective services. As a helper, it is critical for you to know and comply with the mandated reporting laws for your locale.

In general, the gospel instinct to think the best about someone, particularly a fellow believer, is a good and biblical one. But in situations of abuse, speaking of any good you see in oppressors can feed into their sense of "rightness" and fuel the blindness that must ultimately be acknowledged if they are to come to repentance. Much harm has been done in the church, particularly to women in abusive marriages and to childhood victims of sexual abuse, by leaders who didn't take seriously their allegations of abuse. Of course, no person is *all* bad or completely depraved. But that must not be used as a theological smokescreen to ignore pressing issues.[2]

---

2. Helpful resources for leaders in the church include Darby A. Strickland, *Is It Abuse? A Biblical Guide to Identifying Domestic Abuse and Helping Victims* (Phillipsburg, NJ: P & R, 2020); Deepak Reju, *On Guard: Preventing and Responding to Child Abuse at Church* (Greensboro, NC: New Growth Press, 2014); Chris Moles, *The Heart of Domestic Abuse: Gospel Solutions for Men Who Use Control and Violence in the Home* (Bemidji, MN: Focus Publishing, 2015).

Depending on the severity, self-destructive sin patterns such as addictions may require immediate action as well. By analogy, if someone is careening out of control toward the edge of a cliff, you warn them by yelling and screaming, even tackling them if necessary to prevent a fall to their death. You wouldn't simply say, "That's a nice scenic path you've chosen, with a wonderful view of the sea" and hope they come to their senses. Rescue from true danger takes precedence here over any affirmations of good you see.

A pastor I know had a Christian friend of their family stay with them after he left an inpatient rehabilitation facility for heroin addiction, prompted by an overdose that nearly had led to his death. When the pastor found evidence of recent heroin use within his home several months later, he made arrangements for the friend to enter a different treatment program. It was not a time to celebrate past sobriety nor the man's standing with Jesus, but to intervene forthrightly to protect his friend—and the pastor's young family.

Intervening without an initial focus on the good is also important when someone is in imminent danger of ending his life by suicide, as we saw at the beginning of this chapter. This high-risk situation requires crisis intervention. Preserving the life of a friend, family member, or counselee becomes the highest priority. Doing so can put you at odds with the person. My counselee Glen refused to go to the hospital voluntarily to ensure his safety in the moment, thus requiring me to arrange an involuntary psychiatric hospitalization, which was one of the hardest things I had done in ministry to that point. As he was led away by the police, he angrily said to me, "If I had known this was going to happen, I would never have mentioned the gun." I figured my relationship with him was over. However, months later he returned to thank me for my care, and we continued to meet periodically after that.

These exceptions notwithstanding, make it your practice as you interact with others to notice the good—love the person as a saint. When you do that, you reflect God himself, who reminds his people again and again of their identity and the redemptive blessings associated with it. Even in ministry situations when confrontation is needed urgently, we should challenge others with an attitude of humility—for there go I, but for the grace of God (Galatians 6:1).

We have seen throughout this portion of the book the critical importance of moving toward our brothers and sisters as saints united to Jesus Christ. It's hard to live with purpose if you don't know who you are! We so easily forget our identity and need frequent reminders from Scripture and from fellow saints. With this foundational aspect of ministry in place, we turn now to Part 3 of this book, where I'll explore how to minister to others as sufferers.

Part 3:
Loving Others as
Sufferers

Chapter 11

LEARNING THE HARD WAY

My wife and I didn't sleep for nine years. That's a *bit* of an exaggeration, but it reflects the reality of our daughter's multi-year struggle with going to bed and sleeping through the night. From the time we adopted her at ten months of age until she turned ten years old, we dreaded the setting of the sun. Putting her down was sometimes a two-hour marathon replete with crying and tantrums (hers, not ours, for the most part). Exhausted, she would finally fall asleep, only to pop up in bed as we unsuccessfully tiptoed across the minefield of squeaky floorboards in her room. And once asleep, she slept fitfully, waking up several times during the night. As young and inexperienced parents, we were determined to win this battle and not let her come into our room to sleep. It got so bad at some points that my wife and I took every other night as the one on call—one of us would attend to Lydia, the other would sleep with earplugs in another room.

Looking back now, I realize that I did not recognize the level of suffering my daughter was experiencing—the trauma of leaving a loving foster family with whom she had bonded for ten months, attaching to new caregivers (who are these people?) and moving to a new culture where the language she had heard daily (Spanish) was not fluently spoken. I was too often frustrated and angry more than I was saddened. And when she was older and the bedtime battles continued to rage on, I tended to view her as disobedient more than as fearful when she wouldn't stay in her bed. No doubt Lydia was strong-willed and resistant (she would readily agree to these descriptions of her now at age twenty!), but I had eyes to see only the "sinner" aspect of her humanity. I did not approach her in the way Hebrews 5:2 describes Israel's high priest: "He can deal gently with the ignorant and wayward, since he himself is beset with weakness." I am a slow learner—and that showed up in my counseling training as well.

SEEING THE SUFFERING AS A FIRST STEP TO HELPING

In my second semester of counseling courses at Westminster Theological Seminary, I took a class called Methods of Biblical Change with Paul Tripp. Paul ended the first class by showing a video of a ministry conversation he had with a man named John. John was an angry man—a blame-shifting, complaining, angry man. We watched about thirty minutes of Paul's conversation with him. Actually, it felt less like a conversation and more like a rant by the counselee. Tripp's homework assignment for the class was to write answers to these questions: How would you approach John? Where would you go for the second half of the time together?

Here was my thought process: This guy was clearly blind to his sin. I figured that no matter what I said, he wouldn't come back for more of my exceptional wisdom, so it was now or never.

I'd likely only have one shot with the guy, so I decided to let him have it—on paper at least! He needed me to open his blind eyes to the folly of his sin. I could smell the idols of his heart a mile away and lobbed mortar after mortar of biblical truth to blow up his self-oriented ways of living. I thought I was well on my way to becoming an "instrument in the hands of the Redeemer," but in reality, I was more like a blunt object of destruction in my own hands![1]

I'll never forget what Tripp said at the start of the second class: "It's important that you begin by connecting with this man's pain as a first step to helping him. Otherwise he may never return." Ouch! Guilty as charged.

My takeaway was this: while it was certainly true that John manifested clear sin in his life, there were other aspects of his experience that I had failed to notice—most notably the extent of suffering in his life. Understanding a person's suffering is critical for having a fruitful and God-honoring ministry to others. Remember, most people seek help from others because they are suffering and need hope. Whether in everyday family relationships or small groups at church or the counseling office, you will come face-to-face with suffering. So, let's begin with how Scripture models love and understanding to people as sufferers.

---

1. See Paul David Tripp, *Instruments in the Redeemer's Hands: People in Need of Change Helping People in Need of Change* (Phillipsburg, NJ: P & R Publishing, 2002).

Chapter 12

SCRIPTURE SPEAKS TO SUFFERERS

Suffering invades every nook and cranny of our lives. Each day, hardship bombards us or someone we know. A friend in his mid-thirties is diagnosed with Stage IV lung cancer. Dementia steals your elderly mother's vitality. A coworker's previously healthy husband fights for his life after what should have been a routine surgery. Your niece dies of the coronavirus. You don't receive the financial aid you need to attend college. Chronic pain hampers mobility. An adult daughter rejects the faith. A young son is diagnosed on the autistic spectrum. You are downsized out of a job.

In addition to these life-altering trials, there are the daily inconveniences and disappointments of living in a fallen world. The dog howls at 3 a.m., interrupting your sleep for the third night in a row. You drop your new phone, cracking the glass. You need new brakes for the car. The items on your "to do" list multiply, despite your best efforts. Your three-year-old's GI bug becomes the gift that keeps on giving to the rest of the family. Each challenge, in and of itself, is not necessarily life-dominating. But taken together, cumulatively, they form a wearying mosaic of suffering that threatens to erode joy and confidence in the Lord. Nothing is the way it should be. Even our best moments of gladness, joy, and beauty fade. No wonder Job exclaimed, "man is born to trouble as the sparks fly upward" (Job 5:7).

Given the ubiquity of suffering, we often alternate between putting our head in the sand in a posture of naïve optimism (*Maybe I'll be spared*) and living with a foreboding sense of dread (*When will the next shoe of suffering drop?*). Neither posture is biblical. Neither posture prepares us to meet our own suffering with integrity or to walk well with our family, friends, neighbors, and counselees who also experience the relentless ebb and flow of suffering.

This is why we need to see how God speaks to sufferers. This will strengthen us to respond in faith-filled ways to the inevitability of suffering—and finally, to death itself—in our own lives and in the lives of those we love. I am becoming increasingly convinced (now in my late fifties) that my Christian growth rises or falls in concert with the way I view and respond to hardship. I desperately need biblical perspective. As I did earlier in the Saint section, I want to give an overall biblical orientation to suffering before digging into a particular passage.

THE SUFFERING OF GOD'S PEOPLE IS FRONT AND CENTER IN SCRIPTURE

Just as the Bible speaks to saints, the Bible speaks to sufferers. The Bible is full of comfort and perspective for God's people, who have experienced the curses of pain, toil, and death as a result of the fall (Genesis 3:16–19). Moses describes our lot this way: "The years of our life are seventy, or even by reason of strength eighty; yet their span is but toil and trouble; they are soon gone, and we fly away" (Psalm 90:10). The apostle Paul notes that "in this tent [our bodies] we groan, longing to put on our heavenly dwelling" (2 Corinthians 5:2). It's not just us groaning: "the whole creation has been groaning together in the pains of childbirth until now. And not only the creation, but we ourselves, who have the firstfruits of the Spirit, groan inwardly as we wait eagerly for adoption as sons, the redemption of our bodies" (Romans 8:22–23).

"Groaning until glory" is actually a biblical description of the Christian life. The suffering of God's people is front and center throughout Scripture. But also highlighted is God's comfort to his people in the particular moments of their suffering, as well as his promise to bring an end to all suffering, ultimately through the life, death, and resurrection of Jesus Christ.

How do we see God moving toward his suffering people in the pages of Scripture? Psalm 22:24 summarizes an overall pattern you see throughout the Bible: "For he has not despised or abhorred the affliction of the afflicted, and he has not hidden his face from him, but has heard, when he cried to him." God listens to the afflicted. He doesn't turn away in embarrassment or impatience or powerlessness, as we sometimes do.

I live just outside of Philadelphia. The roads are generally overcrowded, and there are frequent accidents. What always happens after an accident? People slow down and look. This is the so-called "gawker delay." We humans are curious about suffering from a distance. But put us up close and personal with suffering, and we find it hard to move toward it, to look fully at its horror. Like the priest and the Levite in the parable of the good Samaritan (Luke 10:25–37), we stay on the other side of the road and avoid the complicated mess of another's suffering. God, on the other hand, does not hide his face. He moves toward sufferers with compassion, and most importantly, he enters into their experience.

JESUS CAME TO SUFFER AND TO RELIEVE SUFFERING

Remembering that the Son of God became incarnate and endured the suffering of a fallen world, fully identifying with human hardship, is a critical perspective to have before us as we consider what it means to love sufferers well. There are two primary strands of teaching on suffering in the New Testament.[1] First, God desires to relieve the suffering that arose as a result of the fall. Consider how Mark 1 describes the activities of Jesus's ministry: teaching, exorcising demons, healing those with various diseases, praying, and cleansing a leper. In Acts, Peter put it this way to Cornelius:

> God anointed Jesus of Nazareth with the Holy Spirit and with power. He went about doing good and healing all who were oppressed by the devil, for God was with him. (Acts 10:38)

Clearly a mark of God's in-breaking kingdom is the relief of suffering. As the Christmas hymn "Joy to the World" reminds us, Jesus "comes to make his blessings flow far as the curse is found." Relief of suffering is a good and necessary thing. This is where history is going; in the new heavens and earth, there will be no crying or pain (Revelation 21:4). So, when we seek

---

1. The remainder of this chapter is adapted from my book, *Descriptions and Prescriptions: A Biblical Perspective on Psychiatric Diagnoses and Medications* (Greensboro, NC: New Growth Press, 2017), 73–78.

to bring relief from suffering now, we are in step with God's plan of redemption. As the Puritan Jeremiah Burroughs said, contentment is "not opposed to all lawful seeking for help in different circumstances, nor endeavoring simply to be delivered out of present afflictions by the use of lawful means."[2] There is nothing wrong with seeking relief from present suffering and helping others to do the same. According to Scripture, we are doing God's work when we seek to relieve suffering.

GOD IS AT WORK IN OUR SUFFERING

The second strand of teaching on suffering in the New Testament is that God plans to redeem believers' suffering through their union with Jesus, the Suffering Servant. Paul calls this "participation in [Jesus's] sufferings" (Philippians 3:10, NIV). Because we are "in Christ," God is at work in the midst of our suffering, conforming us to the image of Christ. Our suffering is the very gateway to experiencing his resurrection power and glory. This is such an important New Testament perspective that I want to slow down and mention several passages where this teaching is central:

> [T]hat I may know him and the power of his resurrection, and may share his sufferings, becoming like him in his death, that by any means possible I may attain the resurrection from the dead. (Philippians 3:10–11)

> The Spirit himself bears witness with our spirit that we are children of God, and if children, then heirs—heirs of God and fellow heirs with Christ, provided we suffer

---

2. Jeremiah Burroughs, *The Rare Jewel of Christian Contentment* (Carlisle, UK: The Banner of Truth Trust, 1964), 22.

with him in order that we may also be glorified with him. (Romans 8:16–17)

Beloved, do not be surprised at the fiery trial when it comes upon you to test you, as though something strange were happening to you. But rejoice insofar as you share Christ's sufferings, that you may also rejoice and be glad when his glory is revealed. (1 Peter 4:12–13)

Now I rejoice in my sufferings for your sake, and in my flesh I am filling up what is lacking in Christ's afflictions for the sake of his body, that is, the church. (Colossians 1:24)

But he said to me, "My grace is sufficient for you, for my power is made perfect in weakness." Therefore I will boast all the more gladly of my weaknesses, so that the power of Christ may rest upon me. For the sake of Christ, then, I am content with weaknesses, insults, hardships, persecutions, and calamities. For when I am weak, then I am strong. (2 Corinthians 12:9–10)[3]

Former seminary professor Richard B. Gaffin Jr. sums up these passages this way:

It is so natural for us to associate suffering only with the delay of Christ's second coming and to view suffering only in the light of what we do not yet have in Christ; but when this happens, we have lost sight of the critical fact that in the New Testament, Christian suffering is always seen within the context of the coming of the

---

3. Other passages include Romans 8:16–25, 2 Corinthians 1:8–9, 2 Corinthians 4, and James 1:2–4.

kingdom of God in power and as a manifestation of the resurrection life of Jesus.[4]

Gaffin is highlighting the truth that God is at work redemptively in the midst of our sufferings by virtue of our being united with the One whose suffering ultimately led to resurrection and glory. We walk in the very footsteps of Jesus—suffering, followed by glory.

This gives us hope. God sees and knows our suffering. His Word shows that suffering is not the end of the story. He intends to overrule and transform suffering in our lives, just as he used the Cross as an instrument to usher in resurrection life for Jesus. Our suffering elder brother Jesus Christ has gone before us; we are not alone in our hardships. With this biblical perspective on suffering as a foundation, let's drill down more specifically into how God meets us in our suffering and how we can do the same with others.

---

4. Richard B. Gaffin Jr., "The Usefulness of the Cross," *Westminster Theological Journal* 41, no. 2 (1979): 229–46. Also available online at http:// www.newhopefairfax.org/images/Gaffin_Usefulness_of_the_Cross.pdf

Chapter 13

HOW GOD LOVES SUFFERERS: A BIBLICAL EXAMPLE

I recall a conversation I had with a friend years ago that centered on the behavioral difficulties my wife and I were having with our young daughter. After pouring out my heart about my sense of failure as a parent and the fear and perplexity that plagued me, he said, "Well, did you ever think about spanking her?" Not helpful! It's so easy to go wrong in caring for the suffering. To speak when it would be better to listen. To offer simplistic advice. To fail to say something potentially meaningful out of fear. And so on. Thankfully, Scripture speaks richly to the problem of suffering and how to minister to sufferers who may be overwhelmed and discouraged.

Entire books of the Bible are written to suffering communities—Lamentations, Ezekiel, Haggai, Hebrews, 1 Peter, Revelation, to name a few. Yet *every* book in the Bible has something to say that is relevant for our suffering. No one passage of Scripture gives us a complete template for ministry to suffering people. No portion of Scripture says everything we need to know about affliction in order to bring hope and consolation to a suffering brother or sister. But let's look at one passage in particular that begins to flesh out some important notes to strike as we come alongside sufferers.

One passage that shows how God loves and speaks to sufferers is Revelation 2:8–11. We can use it to guide us in ministering to suffering people. In the early chapters of Revelation, Jesus addresses each of the seven churches in Asia. Our passage is the message to the church in Smyrna:

> "And to the angel of the church in Smyrna write: 'The words of the first and the last, who died and came to life. I know your tribulation and your poverty (but you are rich) and the slander of those who say that they are Jews and are not, but are a synagogue of Satan. Do not fear what you are about to suffer. Behold, the devil is about to throw some of you into prison, that you may be tested, and for ten days you will have tribulation. Be faithful unto death, and I will give you the crown of life. He who has an ear, let him hear what the Spirit says to the churches. The one who conquers will not be hurt by the second death.'"

What do we notice here that helps us minister to those who are suffering? In this short passage, there are actually seven important aspects to observe and model in our relationships and counseling.

THE MESSAGE IS FROM JESUS

First, the message is from Jesus himself. He is presented not only as the exalted one who is the Alpha and Omega, the first and the last, he is also presented as the one who suffered and died—and came to life again. This is the Jesus about whom the writer of Hebrews says, "he had to be made like his brothers in every respect, so that he might become a merciful and faithful high priest in the service of God" (Hebrews 2:17; see also Hebrews 2:10). His own personal suffering means that he is not detached from the suffering of his people. Any words of consolation we give to others ultimately begin with him. Paul captures this in 2 Corinthians 1:5. "For as we share abundantly in Christ's sufferings, so through Christ we share abundantly in comfort too."

JESUS KNOWS THEIR SPECIFIC AFFLICTIONS

Second, Jesus knows the afflictions of the people at Smyrna, not in some generic way, but very specifically. He knows their tribulation and their poverty. He knows about the suffering caused by slander from others. Likewise, Jesus knows the particular suffering experienced by each church mentioned in Revelation 2:1–3:22. As I previously highlighted, he also knows their suffering because he himself has experienced what it is like to be afflicted, and even to "be faithful unto death."

JESUS DOES NOT COMPARE THEIR SUFFERING TO OTHERS

Third, Jesus doesn't compare their suffering with the suffering in the other churches. The message is not, "Look, I know you've got it rough, but consider those folks in Ephesus. Just be glad you're not experiencing what they are!" Have you ever minimized or maximized someone's sufferings in comparison to your own or others? Consider how that hampers ministry. If you think your friend or counselee's suffering is relatively minor compared to your own (or others you've counseled), you will lack compassion and will exhibit an impatience with their struggle.

If you view another's suffering as so much more than your own ("What could *I* say or do that would make any difference?"), you may shy away from even approaching them. And that leaves them isolated and alone, and you have missed an opportunity to be used by God. You don't see that kind of suffering hierarchy here in Revelation or elsewhere in Scripture. God approaches his people individually, mindful of the specific tears they shed.

JESUS DOES NOT OFFER A REASON FOR THEIR TROUBLE

Fourth, Jesus offers no explanation for their suffering. That is, God does not reveal his inscrutable and specific purposes for their particular suffering at this particular time. He does highlight the role of the devil in their suffering—"the devil is about to throw some of you into prison"—but this is not the same as a full-blown explanation for their affliction.

JESUS'S ENCOURAGEMENT RESHAPES THEIR EXPERIENCE

Fifth, he brings words of encouragement, which are meant to shape their reality in the midst of their suffering. It's as if Jesus is saying, "I know you are truly afflicted and poverty-stricken, and I care about what you are experiencing. But I also don't want you to forget that you possess riches that cannot be taken away." During his earthly ministry, Jesus brought similar encouragement to his anxious disciples by reminding them that they had been given the kingdom by God the Father, "a treasure in the heavens that does not fail" (Luke 12:33).

JESUS IS WITH THEM IN SUFFERING

Sixth, Jesus says, "Do not fear." This is the most common call from God in the pages of Scripture. This doesn't have the feel of "oh you of little faith," but rather of a parent comforting a child who has experienced a nightmare in the middle of the night. "Don't be afraid, I know you're scared. But I'm here with you." In his ministry on earth, Jesus put literal flesh on the promise of Isaiah 41:10a, "Fear not, for I am with you." Through the presence of the Holy Spirit, Jesus remains with his followers even after he has ascended (John 14:16–18; Matthew 28:20b).

JESUS GIVES THEM HOPE

Seventh, Jesus leaves them with further hope and a call to persevere: "I will give you the crown of life." This is what the finish line looks like! This echoes what Paul says in 2 Timothy 4:7–8:

> I have fought the good fight, I have finished the race, I have kept the faith. Henceforth there is laid up for me the crown of righteousness, which the Lord, the righteous judge, will award to me on that Day, and not only to me but also to all who have loved his appearing.

In Christ, we cannot be hurt by the "second death." The "second death" refers to the final judgment and condemnation of those who are not believers in Jesus Christ (see Revelation 20:11–14; 21:8). All people, believers and unbelievers alike, suffer a first death (physical death). The second death is eternal death (separation from God for all eternity) and is reserved for unbelievers.

Carefully considering how the Lord himself moves toward and speaks comfort to his suffering people shows us the way forward in the difficult and delicate conversations we have as we minister to other believers who are suffering. There are many ways that Christians can (and have) gone wrong in their approach to sufferers, but the words of Jesus are a sure guide for navigating these deep waters. Let's consider in the next chapter several specific ways to apply Jesus's approach—which takes suffering seriously and offers timely biblical hope and comfort—in our own ministry to others.

Chapter 14

MINISTRY PRIORITIES FOR LOVING SUFFERERS

My children have observed that I've become more serious as I have gotten older. I believe they are on to something. It reflects the truth that I have seen many people—friends, family, church members, and counselees—suffer over the years. Some have died of cancer, others from heroin overdose. Marriages have ended. Strokes have brought the need for 24/7 care. Elderly parents have died after agonizing hospital stays. A routine surgery has led to unexpected and devastating consequences. A cherished business has failed, resulting in long-lasting financial ripples. I know I am not alone in this. The experiences of suffering in this life feel, at the very least, like the disquiet of a brewing storm, more often like choppy seas that bounce and bruise, and sometimes like a raging tempest that destroys everything in its path. This spectrum of suffering is common to us all. How then, in the midst of all this suffering, do we minister to others like Jesus did to the church of Smyrna?

TAKE THE SUFFERING OF OTHERS SERIOUSLY

First and foremost, we acknowledge deeply the reality and difficulty of suffering. Because God himself repeatedly speaks to his people about their suffering, we are always attentive to this sobering reality in our ministry to others. Scripture never shies away from Jesus's stark reminder, "In the world you will have tribulation" (John 16:33b). While it is true that Jesus goes on to say, "But take heart; I have overcome the world" (John 16:33c), you never hear him scold, "Buck up, it's not as bad as you think it is." Actually, it *is* that bad. So bad in fact that the Son of God had to suffer and die to bring the promise of suffering's demise. The gospel is the good news that Jesus has come to renew all things as "far as the curse is found." And that includes the misery of suffering.

When we are faced with either immense suffering or the constant drip, drip, drip of everyday problems and disappointments, there is a temptation to either numb ourselves in resignation or to aggressively try and fix what's wrong by wielding whatever control and power we can muster within ourselves. Scripture models neither approach, but instead directs us to our Savior with whom we are united, in both his suffering and his comfort. So, one implication for ministry is that we never shy away from the ever-present reality of suffering, nor try to minimize it. Living with this clear-eyed gaze on suffering prompts us to engage the One who fully understands.

WORK HARD TO UNDERSTAND THE DETAILS

Second, we work hard to understand (as Jesus did) the particulars of suffering. To do that, we need to be present and listen well. We can't truly feel the weight of another's suffering without knowing that person's story, and we can't know it without listening. And asking questions. And listening some more. We want to be able to say, "I *know* your afflictions." And sometimes that listening is uncomfortable because we will hear doubt and raw, un-sanitized emotions.

God himself gives us these same kinds of words in the Psalms, particularly the psalms of lament. For example, Psalm 88 ends with "darkness is my closest friend" (NIV). In this example, the psalmist doesn't repent of or qualify his statement. It simply hangs there without any attempt to correct his experience, and without a footnote that gives a full-orbed and nuanced theology of suffering. Of course, we have more than Psalm 88 in the Psalter! But as you listen to someone's story and are trying to fully understand it, be careful not to move away from the pain too quickly. In many places, Scripture lingers in lament. Give people a safe environment to give voice to their suffering and struggle—to you and to the Lord.

This is true even if a person's emotional or physical suffering is primarily a consequence of their personal sin, particularly in the past. You never hear God say, "Well, too bad. You should have listened to me before you made that foolish choice." Rather, God remains responsive to the cry of his people in their distress, even distress of their own making (see Judges 2:16–18, as well as many psalms). The apostle Paul no doubt carried with him the weighty reality of his earlier life (1 Corinthians 15:9; 1 Timothy 1:15), but he highlighted the grace of Jesus overflowing for him (1 Timothy 1:14). If a person is suffering due to ongoing sin patterns, we take seriously the misery caused by his sin *and* call him to repentance. In either case, the mercies of God are available and renewed each morning (Lamentations 3:22–24).

DON'T PRESUME YOU KNOW THE REASON(S) FOR SUFFERING

A third implication for ministry from Revelation 2:8–11 is that we do not presume to know exactly what God is up to in the midst of someone's suffering. It is true that Scripture speaks about the redemption of suffering in our lives. Trials of various kinds produce steadfastness that culminates in maturity (James 1:3–4). The apostle Paul highlights that "suffering produces endurance, and endurance produces character, and character produces hope" (Romans 5:3b–4). These passages and the ones that demonstrate our union with Jesus in his suffering and glory are critical for gaining perspective in the midst of suffering. But we should not confidently assert these are *the* reasons why a particular person is suffering. Don't equate the endpoint of suffering (steadfastness, hope) with the inscrutable purposes of God for *this* particular person's suffering. Sometimes a person, either in the midst of suffering or reflecting on a past season of suffering will say, "This is what God was up to in my life during that time." Such conclusions are likely born out of much prayerful reflection in the midst of their own stories. But we should be more tentative in our assertions, knowing that we are not able to truly penetrate the mystery of God's will and purposes.

SHARE BIBLICAL ENCOURAGEMENT AND HOPE

A fourth implication for ministry is that our counsel to the sufferer brings biblical perspective and clarity. Although we come alongside the person, incarnating the presence of Christ and listening well, we ultimately do more than commiserate. Jesus brought words of encouragement and hope to the people of Smyrna that were meant to help them persevere in the present struggle. This is tricky, of course. Bringing biblical perspective, without the person sensing that you do indeed understand their struggle, will fall flat, at best, and at worst will add further discouragement. At the same time, I know that in my own times of suffering I need more than someone to simply agree, again and again, that life is hard. It is indeed, but how does the risen One meet me and carry me forward? I need someone to encourage me with those realities. I need a corrective lens when all I see is blurry. God enters our suffering, and he transforms it. This helps us (and those we minister to) take heart. I need to know there is truly a good ending to this story, or I will not have the strength to journey on.

Christina Rosetti's poem, "Up-hill," beautifully captures this reality:

> Does the road wind up-hill all the way?
>> Yes, to the very end.
> Will the day's journey take the whole long day?
>> From morn to night, my friend.
>
> But is there for the night a resting-place?
>> A roof for when the slow dark hours begin.
> May not the darkness hide it from my face?
>> You cannot miss that inn.
>
> Shall I meet other wayfarers at night?
>> Those who have gone before.
> Then must I knock, or call when just in sight?
>> They will not keep you standing at that door.
>
> Shall I find comfort, travel-sore and weak?
>> Of labour you shall find the sum.
> Will there be beds for me and all who seek?
>> Yea, beds for all who come.[1]

---

1. Christina Rosetti, "Up-hill," Poetry Foundation, https://www. poetryfoundation.org/poems/45002/up-hill.

We and those we minister to often find the way to be an uphill climb. But a welcoming place of lodging and rest awaits.

The apostle Peter captures the journey this way: "And after you have suffered a little while, the God of all grace, who has called you to his eternal glory in Christ, will himself restore, confirm, strengthen, and establish you" (1 Peter 5:10). The truth that we will experience eternal glory, restoration, confirmation, strength, and firm establishment gives hope to press forward when the path is marked with suffering. We want to be able to communicate that hope to those we minister to. No doubt this takes wisdom and courage. We need wisdom because we don't want to rush in with a few verses disconnected from the particulars of the person's suffering. At the same time, we should have courage to speak with quiet confidence the words from Scripture that God intends to bring comfort and hope. There is "a time to keep silence and time to speak" (Ecclesiastes 3:7b).

Paying attention to how Jesus loved the people of Smyrna establishes the ministry priorities we explored in this chapter. But what does it look like to live out this framework as we come alongside sufferers? Let's get even more specific. In the next two chapters, we'll discuss how to approach fellow sufferers in everyday life and in more formal counseling situations.

Chapter 15

HOW WE LOVE SUFFERERS: EVERYDAY EXAMPLES

When he was younger, my son had frequent nightmares and he would come into our bedroom at night. He was very nice about it—tiptoeing ever so quietly into our room and standing bent over one of us until we would awaken with a start and see his staring face inches from ours! What didn't work at those times was giving him a rational explanation and putting him back to bed. He would be back within minutes. What *was* helpful was crawling into bed with him. My presence or the presence of my wife Jody was what mattered. We communicated, "Don't be afraid" not only with words, but also by being there with him. The same is true of Jesus. His call not to fear is wedded to his very presence. He encourages his disciples with the promise of the Holy Spirit, "I will not leave you as orphans; I will come to you. . . . Let not your hearts be troubled, neither let them be afraid" (John 14:18, 27b). Presence matters—in God's ministry to us and in our ministry to others. It's of primary importance simply to be present when ministering to someone who is suffering. As a husband, parent, friend, and counselor I've found that a ministry of presence generally precedes a ministry of words.

Here's another example. My son is an avid soccer player, and when he is on the field, he has no fear. One time several seasons ago, he didn't get up after a fall. As the manager motioned me on to the field, I knew something was terribly wrong. One look at his arm told me all I needed to know—he had broken both of the bones in his forearm. What did he need at that moment? Questions about how it happened? Reassurances that he would be playing in no time? An anatomy lesson? "You see son, there are two bones in the forearm, the ulna and the radius and it looks like you broke both of them." Correction? "How many times have I told you to try and stay on your feet?" Theologizing? "Son, James tells us to 'count it all joy . . . when you meet trials of various kinds, for you know that the testing of your faith produces steadfastness' (James 1:2–3)." Absolutely not. What he needed was for me to sit with him and wait calmly and patiently for the ambulance. To lay my hand on him and to assure him of my presence and Jesus's presence with him in the midst of the pain. Often this incarnational ministry of presence is the very first aspect of ministry to people, for both formal and informal settings. And it serves to validate the reality and difficulty of the person's suffering.

In addition to this ministry of presence, how do we deeply understand the particular experience of those who are suffering and initially respond to them? At least four things come to mind:

- listen patiently (and have eyes to see more than sinful responses in the midst of people's suffering),
- ask questions,

- pray, and
- provide hope and practical help

Let's elaborate on these.

LISTEN WITH PATIENCE

Catherine Woodiwiss, a writer who experienced major loss, says, "Trauma is terrible. What we need in the aftermath is a friend who can swallow her own discomfort and fear, sit beside us, and just let it be terrible for a while."[1] We are often less patient with a sufferer's process of confusion and lament than God is. Sometimes we want to rush the process because it's uncomfortable for *us*. Who wants to see a loved one in agony, teetering into bitterness?

Imagine your friend, following the death of his wife, saying, "Meanwhile, where is God? This is one of the most disquieting symptoms. When you are happy, so happy that you have no sense of needing Him, so happy that you are tempted to feel His claims upon you as an interruption, if you remember yourself and turn to Him with gratitude and praise, you will be—or so it feels—welcomed with open arms. But go to Him when your need is desperate, when all other help is vain, and what do you find? A door slammed in your face, and a sound of bolting and double bolting on the inside. After that, silence. You may as well turn away. . . . Why is He so present a commander in our time of prosperity and so very absent a help in time of trouble?" Does it make you squirm a bit to listen to those words? Do you fear your friend's loss of faith? Do you want to jump to God's defense?

---

1. Catherine Woodiwiss, "A New Normal: Ten Things I've Learned about Trauma," *Sojourners*, January 13, 2014, https://sojo.net/articles/new-normal-ten-things-ive-learned-about-trauma.

These words came from the pen of C. S. Lewis following the death of his wife, Joy Davidman—words recorded in his journal, which became the book *A Grief Observed*.[2] Throughout the book you see Lewis wrestling with his questions and doubts. His struggle is not fully resolved by the end of the book, but he is able to say, "I have gradually been coming to feel that the door is no longer shut and bolted."[3] For the friend sitting next to Lewis, patient listening is in order, just as God patiently listens to the questions and agonies of the psalmists. Would *you* try to sanitize C. S. Lewis's sorrow and remind him of what he wrote about God in the previous years? "C'mon, Jack, after all the brilliant things you've said about God, can't you do better than that?" Maybe we wouldn't have dared to say that to C. S. Lewis, but we do misstep frequently in our care of others. We often fail to listen patiently, just as Job's friends did, friends whom Job referred to as "miserable comforters" (Job 16:2).

Even if time has elapsed and you worry that a suffering person is stuck in self-pity, bitterness, and unbelief, you must carefully lead the person to a deeper self-awareness and to a realization of the truth and mercy of God. People often ask real and raw questions, especially early in a grieving and suffering process, but they are not necessarily looking for you to provide an "answer" just at that moment. But with time, if the questions, doubts, and confusion remain, and if you have been a faithful and patient helper, perhaps the person will trust you to help wrestle through these questions. We have to be sensitive to what this particular person needs.

A friend who was forced to resign from her job by her unreasonable employer initially needed compassion and

2. C. S. Lewis, *A Grief Observed* (New York: Harper Collins, 1994), 5–6.

3. Lewis, *A Grief Observed*, 46.

unwearied listening. Over time, as her bitterness and her doubts about God's providential care grew, she needed (and accepted) help to wrestle through how her heart had twisted grief into resentment and smoldering anger toward God. She trusted my questions and observations because she knew I cared deeply and had been willing to lament alongside her in her loss.

So, don't mandate that the person's response to suffering be cleaned up or sterilized before you come alongside him or her. The psalms of lament don't show that. Generally they don't read like this: "Since I've finally resolved all my anger and doubts and grief in private, now I can publicly recount God's faithfulness and purposes in the midst of suffering." No, in many psalms the honest wrestling plays out right before our eyes (and the eyes of God). It's encouraging that God models patience in listening to his people's cries, tears, questions, and doubts. Can we trust that God has our friends and counselees in his strong grip, despite their flailings and failings? Putting our faith in God and his good care for those who are suffering allows us to be patient listeners as they share their sorrows.

ASK QUESTIONS

With listening comes the importance of asking good questions that communicate concern and care. Merely nodding and murmuring, "uh huh" communicates, "Thanks for sharing, but I really haven't heard much of what you said." Rather, one way we show love toward sufferers in our midst is to ask questions that demonstrate genuine interest. People might open up about their struggles on their own without someone asking how they're doing, but often they don't. And *we* model vulnerability when we respond to questions about our well-being with more than just, "Fine." At the same time, always consider what is most loving right now for the person in front of you before asking questions. You ask questions not only to gain information, but also (and especially) to build your relationship with them.

Questions that get beyond the facts to how they are experiencing their hardship are key:

- "That sounds really scary. How are you feeling about that?"
- "What are you most worried about?"
- "Who in your life is coming alongside you to help with these challenges?"
- "Is there anything that you have found helpful in the midst of your situation?"

Ed Welch, in his CCEF blog post, "What Not to Say to Those Who Are Suffering," urges caution even in the kinds of questions we may pose to sufferers.[4] He particularly identifies the question, "What is God teaching you?" as a generally unhelpful question since (1) it can communicate condescension; (2) it suggests that suffering is a riddle to be solved; (3) it implies we have done something to warrant the suffering; and (4) it undercuts God's call to all suffering people to simply trust him. Subtly it communicates, "Have you learned your lesson yet?" even if that is not our intent.

I've found that asking, "What can I do to help?" or "What would be most helpful right now?" cuts both ways. On the one hand, it communicates a sense of humility—that is, I don't presume to know what would be most helpful to you right now, so that's why I'm asking. On the other hand, someone in the

_____

4. Ed Welch, "What Not to Say to Those Who Are Suffering," CCEF, February 22, 2010, https://www.ccef.org/resources/blog/what-not-say-those-who-are-suffering.

midst of deep and overwhelming suffering may not even have the energy to formulate a response. They may experience your question as an additional burden, requiring them to come up with solutions in the midst of their suffering.

If you have an idea about how to help, you could simply say, for example, "I would love to make a meal for you and drop it by later this week. Would that be helpful to you, or could I do something else instead?" (Or, if you're in a more formal counseling setting, "I would be happy to call your care group leader to talk about setting up a meal rotation for you. Or we can brainstorm other possibilities that might be more helpful.") Those kinds of responses communicate proactive and thoughtful care, but also the humility to be overruled.

PRAY

Listening and learning the contours of people's struggles lead to honest prayer. This is especially important when others may not feel as though they have the strength to pray for themselves. What do you pray? It's appropriate to ask, "How can I pray for you?" and then, after hearing what the person says, "Could I pray for you right now?"

If the suffering person is not sure how you can pray but is open to you praying, keep it simple. Pray in keeping with how God has revealed himself in Scripture to those who suffer. Intercessory prayer should not be a covert attempt to theologize, teach, or correct, but a heartfelt appeal to the Father of mercies. You are imploring God to pour out his grace and mercy in your friend's time of need. At the same time, biblically grounded prayer does provide perspective, encouragement, and hope for the sufferer. I often pray for specific people in these ways:

Thank you, Lord God, that you see and are moved by Dave's experience of chronic pain. May he know your presence and comfort in the midst of his isolation (based on Psalm 23:4).

Jesus, you wept at Lazarus's tomb. Please be near to Ann, weeping with her in the loss of her dear sister (based on John 11:33–35).

Gracious God, who made heaven and earth, provide help to Tim now (based on Psalm 121:2).

Father, I'm not even sure what to pray, but I thank you that your Spirit is interceding for us right now as Mary and I cry out before you (based on Romans 8:26).

As you pray, you are also modeling what it looks like to give voice to suffering before God. (I will talk more about this in the next chapter.)

After listening, learning, and praying, do follow up. Recently, I was incredibly blessed by the care of a friend, really an acquaintance I see very infrequently. I had last seen him many months ago after my father had died, but he showed his genuine care for me by asking how my elderly mother was doing now and recalling specific details I had shared with him earlier. I was amazed that he had remembered what I said then, and also took the initiative to ask. We want to encourage others in the same way. If you have trouble remembering conversations, jot a few notes down and incorporate them into your personal times of prayer. You will be more likely to remember to ask about that situation the next time you see that person.

PROVIDE HOPE AND PRACTICAL HELP

The previous steps of care have the real potential to provide hope and encouragement to the suffering person and to orient her toward God. They also lead you to a place of potentially providing tangible and more knowledgeable hands-on help for the sufferer. While it's true that we sometimes run too quickly to try and fix someone's suffering before we understand it, we can still talk with that person about practical ways to relieve their suffering, even as God carries out his redemptive agenda of transformation in the midst of the suffering. We want to avoid a "fix it" mentality, but we also want to avoid a detached "deal with it" mentality.

Loving a suffering friend or family member involves caring enough to talk about practical means of care that serve to relieve suffering. We want to avoid what James 2:15–16 describes: "If a brother or sister is poorly clothed and lacking in daily food, and one of you says to them, 'Go in peace, be warmed and filled,' without giving them the things needed for the body, what good is that?" The apostle John speaks in a similar way: "But if anyone has the world's goods and sees his brother in need, yet closes his heart against him, how does God's love abide in him? Little children, let us not love in word or talk but in deed and in truth" (1 John 3:17–18). Love takes a tangible and concrete shape. The question we looked at previously, "What can I do to help?" moves in that direction.

Although this book is primarily about loving and helping one another in the context of intentional and constructive conversation, our word ministry should be associated with deeds that exemplify the mercy, kindness, and justice of God (Micah 6:6). We should always be asking, "How can I be a good neighbor to this suffering person?" (Luke 10:25–37). As we saw earlier, Scripture certainly does not prohibit seeking relief and practical solutions in the midst of suffering, even as it highlights God's presence and consolation in our experience of suffering.

Notice that all I have been saying about ministry to suffering believers also applies to how we love unbelievers. The same movements of love—taking their suffering seriously, asking questions to understand the particulars of their afflictions, and offering to pray all apply. In fact, this level of personal care, accompanied by tangible deed ministry, often sparks the spiritual interest of suffering unbelievers and opens the door to conversations that move in a gospel-centered direction.

Pain gets our attention, for believers and unbelievers alike, and directs our gaze toward the One who, through Jesus Christ, is overcoming all brokenness and suffering originating from Adam and Eve's tragic rebellion. As C. S. Lewis famously wrote, "Pain insists upon being attended to. God whispers to us in our pleasures, speaks in our conscience, but shouts in our pain: it is His megaphone to rouse a deaf world."[5] Suffering rightly makes us exclaim, "This is not the way it's supposed to be!" and makes us long for redemption.

I love the way the Bible describes how Jonathan ministered to David in the midst of being on the run from Saul's murderous jealousy: "And Saul's son Jonathan went to David at Horesh and helped him find strength in God" (1 Samuel 23:16, NIV). Being present, listening, asking questions, praying, and providing practical support in the name of Jesus are ways we can all help sufferers find their strength in God. It's simple—and profound. That's what it means to be a caring and intentional friend in everyday life. Let's explore a few other ways we can

---

5. C. S. Lewis, *The Problem of Pain* (New York: Harper Collins, 2001), 91.

love sufferers well in the next chapter, using several counseling examples.

Chapter 16

HOW WE LOVE SUFFERERS: COUNSELING EXAMPLES

Much of my counseling ministry is weighted toward consoling sufferers, particularly in the early stages of meeting together. I counsel primarily in a parachurch context with believers, and many are struggling with anxiety, depression, or doubts about their faith. Leaders I counsel often struggle with burnout and vocational dilemmas. In that sense, many of my counselees are a "bruised reed" and "smoldering wick" (Isaiah 42:3) who require patient and tender care, laced with encouragement. Most people that I counsel I am meeting for the very first time, which generally means I take adequate time to listen to their stories, ask good questions, highlight the good I see God already doing in their lives (confirming their identity as saints), and find ways to connect them to their Savior who has walked the path of suffering and glory before them.

In everyday relationships or in a setting where ministry leaders already know people well (pastors and their flock, small group leaders and their members, etc.), relational capital and trust has built up over time, and so ministry is less linear and much more organic. To use an electrical circuit analogy, ministry is less "in series" and more "in parallel." The reality of being simultaneously saint, sufferer, and sinner is more at the forefront in those settings.

With someone you know well, a single conversation may touch on all three aspects of life as a believer, in no particular order. Or you may press into an area of sin in a small group member's life precisely because you have had many other points of engagement as saints and sufferers. It is true that for the purposes of this book, these three "parallel" modes of ministry have been somewhat artificially separated into a "series" mode of ministry. However, in a more formal ministry/counseling context where you may be building your relationship for the first time, the serial progression of ministry from saint to sufferer to sinner generally holds true. But as I mentioned earlier in the book, in ministry to believers, both informally and formally, we must never lose sight of their primary identity as saints. This has to remain foundational lest we gravitate toward relating to them *only* in light of their weaknesses and failures.

CONNECTING SCRIPTURE TO SUFFERERS

As I did in the "Saint" section of the book, I will share two counseling examples where the main ministry priority was loving a sufferer. As before, I'll focus on ways of using Scripture explicitly to minister to someone who is suffering.

Ruth is a seventy-two-year-old woman who lost her husband ten months ago after a prolonged decline with early onset Alzheimer's disease, which had been diagnosed eight years earlier. She had cared for him at home over that entire time, and it was particularly grueling over the last three years of his life. Now, nearly a year after his death, she struggles with discouragement and fear. She said to me, "It's been a difficult journey, and I am so weary. I feel like I've run a marathon and survived, but I worry that God will ask me to run another marathon. I'm not sure I will have the strength to run it. Will God throw me another curveball that, this time, I won't be able to hit? I fear I will dishonor him." And she feels guilty for even thinking this way. How would you bring comfort and perspective to this dear woman of God?

What came to my mind in that moment was the story of Elijah in 1 Kings 19. You may remember the basic contours— God has just given Elijah a mighty and miraculous victory over the prophets of Baal (recorded in 1 Kings 18). But Jezebel, King Ahab's wife, vows to put him to death. And what does Elijah do? He runs like a scared rabbit into the wilderness and basically gives up, asking God to take his life (19:3–4). And what does God do? Rebuke him for his lack of faith? "You just saw me defeat 450 prophets of Baal and you're worried about Jezebel?! Get a grip!" No, the Lord recognizes his weariness and allows him both to sleep and to eat—food that God himself has prepared for Elijah (19:6). Notice the kindness of God's ministering angel, "Arise and eat, for the journey is too great for you" (19:7). Then with the strength provided by that food and rest, he travels to Mount Sinai (Horeb) and meets with God.

Is Elijah now strong in faith? Is he in a better frame of mind? No, he's still got Jezebel on the brain! God asks him what he's doing here and Elijah responds, "I have been very jealous for the LORD, the God of hosts. For the people of Israel have forsaken your covenant, thrown down your altars, and killed your prophets with the sword, and I, even I only, am left, and they seek my life, to take it away" (19:10 and repeated again in verse 14). God responds by telling Elijah that in fact, he is not alone—there are 7,000 in Israel who have not forsaken the Lord—and he gives Elijah a three-fold mission to anoint a new king over Syria, a new king over Israel (in place of Ahab), and a new prophet, Elisha, who will succeed Elijah (19:15–18).

What did I want Ruth to notice here as we read through the chapter together and interacted over specific verses? I certainly wanted her to see God's tender care for Elijah in the midst of his weariness and frailty of faith. God did not rebuke him for his fear and for his spiritual, emotional, and physical exhaustion. God came to him not in wind, earthquake, or fire (common powerful manifestations) but in a quiet whisper, or perhaps more accurately, in the sound of silence (19:11–13). And what was God's message? A reminder that he was not alone and that God still had vital ministry for him to do. God would continue to give him exactly what he needed when he needed it.

This was an encouragement to Ruth. Life as a newly single woman remained challenging, but, despite her weariness, she saw that she was not alone. She took heart that God's posture toward her was not one of crossed arms and impatient foot tapping, but of nearness in the midst of battle weariness. Just as God drew near to Elijah, God has drawn even nearer to Ruth through Jesus Christ. While I didn't think of this at the time, I could have more explicitly connected Ruth with the invitation of Jesus in Matthew 11:28–30, "Come to me, all who labor and are heavy laden, and I will give you rest. Take my yoke upon you, and learn from me, for I am gentle and lowly in heart, and you will find rest for your souls. For my yoke is easy, and my burden is light."

Notice that 1 Kings 19 (or Matthew 11 for that matter) has nothing to do with the specific form of suffering called widowhood. Rather, Ruth's experience of weariness and fear in the midst of widowhood was the point of connection between her life and the Scriptures. The passage did indeed speak into her exhaustion and her concern that perhaps God would require too much of her. She drew hope from how God concretely bolstered Elijah in his time of need.

What practical steps followed? How did this passage contribute to Ruth's growth in Christ in the midst of her suffering? She decided to make an appointment with her physician for a routine checkup. You might say, "Huh? I'm not sure I would have applied the passage that way!" But here's why making that appointment was a step of faith. Ruth had been procrastinating, not wanting to schedule a doctor's visit out of fear that something negative would be found and her anxieties of running another marathon (this time related to her own health problems) would be confirmed. But she was encouraged by God's compassionate and persistent ministry and presence to Elijah, which gave her courage to press forward rather than shrink back in fear.

LEARNING TO LAMENT FROM SCRIPTURE

Here's a second example from Ruth's life, also related to ministry in the midst of her suffering. As we spent time together, I realized that she had been hesitant to express her grief to God and others. She felt guilty even acknowledging how difficult the last years of her husband's condition had been for her. She had never really dealt with the cumulative weight of grief and loss associated not only with the care of her chronically ill husband, but also with unmet expectations for what the retirement years of her marriage would look like. In the midst of all her sorrow, she needed to learn how to lament. She needed to view her suffering as legitimate and to cry out to God in the midst of it. She had taken the step of talking with me about it. I wanted her to talk with God about it.

As I mentioned earlier, the Psalms are a rich source of help for those who are suffering. The lament psalms actually make up the largest group of psalms in the entire Psalter, which highlights the priority God places on giving sufferers words to speak back to him in their time of distress.[1] Which psalm might you choose to help Ruth? I settled on Psalm 77, which is one of my favorites. Like so many psalms, it couples honest and heartfelt cries of grief and confusion with confidence in God's covenant faithfulness and love.

The psalm begins with the honest admission that despite crying out to God, the psalmist's soul "refuses to be comforted" (77:2). He is so troubled that he cannot speak (77:4). The psalmist then asks a series of questions that sufferers often wonder about, even if they have not voiced them to anyone else:

"Will the Lord spurn forever,
    and never again be favorable?
Has his steadfast love forever ceased?
    Are his promises at an end for all time?
Has God forgotten to be gracious?
    Has he in anger shut up his compassion?" (77:7–9)

The psalm takes a turn in verses 10–11:

Then I said, "I will appeal to this,
    to the years of the right hand of the Most High."
I will remember the deeds of the Lord;
    yes, I will remember your wonders of old.[2]

---

1. Examples of lament psalms would include 10, 13, 22, 42, 43, 77, and 142, among many others.

2. An alternate rendering of verse 10 (noted in a footnote in the ESV) is "This is my grief: that the right hand of the Most High has changed." This fits especially well with the tenor of the psalm up to this point and captures the confusion and doubts that sufferers often experience amidst

The psalmist then alludes to the powerful work of God in redeeming his people from Egypt, particularly in providing a path for them through the Red Sea (77:19). The psalm ends without an explicit resolution of the psalmist's lament, but it at least implies the redirection of grief toward hope: the God who has acted faithfully in the past for us will meet us in our current distress. This is even more true for believers today, given the life, death, and resurrection of Jesus Christ, in whom all God's promises are "yes" and "Amen" (2 Corinthians 1:20).

What did I want Ruth to see here? God invites us into the messy process of wrestling before him in the midst of our sorrows and hardships. The honest words of the psalmist become our own. This psalm and others gave Ruth the freedom to be in process, to linger with the questions and confusion of verses 7–9 without feeling guilty, even while she sought to direct her laments to her faithful and loving God.

As you work with suffering brothers and sisters, help them lament with the hope that is grounded in the redemptive work of Jesus Christ. Carefully couple grief in the present with confidence drawn from the past work of God and from the promises of his future restoration. "Weeping may tarry for the night, but joy comes with the morning" (Psalm 30:5b). At the same time, it is appropriate for sufferers (like Ruth) to give themselves to the practice of nighttime weeping and not rush to a forced and premature morning joy. Some joys will not dawn until we see Jesus face to face.

One last word here—you can, of course, bring comfort and hope to someone without quoting a particular biblical passage, as I highlighted in the preceding two chapters. Sometimes

---

the dark providences of God. In either case, verse 11 serves as the hinge for the psalm as the psalmist begins to recount the mighty deeds of God in the past.

sitting in silence with a sufferer is exactly what is needed, even in the context of a more formal ministry setting. And sometimes we will simply say, "Jesus knows your pain" without quoting Hebrews 4:15. We need wisdom to know when to speak and what to say to those in the midst of great suffering. We often struggle to do this, so the next chapter will consider some of the barriers to loving sufferers well.

Chapter 17

BARRIERS TO LOVING OTHERS AS SUFFERERS

A member of your small group lingers after everyone else has left. "Could I talk to you about something?" he asks. He proceeds to tell you about his lifelong struggle with same-sex attraction. He shares his pain, his fears, his confusion, his loneliness—and his frustration that your church focuses so much on married couples that singles feel isolated and overlooked. How do you handle the fine china of this young man's life, including his criticisms? If we're honest, sometimes we struggle with ministering to sufferers in helpful ways. Here are seven possible reasons why.

1. We haven't listened long enough to truly grasp the extent of their suffering. The longer we listen, the more thoughtful and helpful our love will be. I have been counseling someone for several years who continues to reveal new layers and intricacies to her lifelong history of physical, emotional, sexual, and spiritual

abuse. Increasingly, we've been able to talk about how she is not defined by her traumas. She's become much more honest about her fears and her shame rather than pointing out the faults of others. She increasingly desires to move toward others in the same way God has moved toward her. She has prayed more for others. This is the Spirit's work that has grown out of her finding space to honestly and repeatedly voice her suffering before God, with the help of several advocates.

2. We want to make things better too quickly for people. We want to fix their problems because we don't like to see loved ones suffer (although sometimes it's because we find that lingering in a place of suffering and lament is uncomfortable for us). While it's appropriate to prayerfully consider possible solutions to a person's struggles, as I mentioned earlier, have you ever rushed to a solution only to be met with a withering look that says, "What I most needed right now was a listening ear, not an answer man"? (Not that this has happened to me of course . . .) Sometimes our attempts to help, whether in word or deed, can feel like applying a Band-Aid on a gaping wound. There's a fine line between hope-filled encouragement based on God's character and promises, and subtly (or not so subtly) communicating, "Get over it."

Pastor and author Zack Eswine writes of the reality of "inconsolable things"—the pains, sorrows, and sufferings that simply will not be resolved or go away until Jesus returns to consummate his kingdom.[1] A "fix it" mentality simply won't work. And as we've seen, while Scripture certainly does not prohibit seeking relief and solutions in the midst of suffering, it highlights God's presence and consolation in the midst of suffering, and often speaks of the redemption God is bringing in the

---

1. Zack Eswine, *The Imperfect Pastor: Discovering Joy in Our Limitations through a Daily Apprenticeship with Jesus* (Wheaton, IL: Crossway, 2015), 96–99.

midst of suffering. The apostle Paul reminds us that outwardly we are wasting away, but inwardly we are being renewed (2 Corinthians 4:16). God is at work in the midst of affliction even when a situation doesn't outwardly change. We pray for our friends and counselees to have ears to hear that perspective at the right time.

3. We're more focused on the sinful ways people are responding to their suffering, so rather than bringing comfort initially, we confront. This was my barrier to loving John, the angry man that Paul Tripp introduced to me in his counseling class. There are, of course, times when a person's grief manifests as anger or other destructive behaviors that put others in harm's way. In those situations, addressing the sin in a direct, compassionate way is important: "I know that you are hurting, but the way you are taking out your anger on everyone around you is destroying relationships with the very people God wants you to draw near to. This has to stop. God has a better way for you to deal with your grief. Let me walk with you to discover it."

I follow Philadelphia sports teams, and the slogan that has marked the rebuilding of the Philadelphia 76ers basketball team over the last few years has been, "trust the process."[2] It was an idea attributed to Sam Hinkie, who served as the Sixers' General Manager from 2013–16. The phrase meant tolerating the short-term tanking of an already mediocre team for the long-term gains of rebuilding a new team from scratch. And it worked. The Sixers were 10–72 in 2015–16, but were 51–31 in 2018–19, making it to the Eastern Conference semifinals two years in a row. As a helper, learn to trust God's process; you can be sure

2. Max Rappaport, "The Definitive History of 'Trust the Process,'" *Bleacher Report*, Turner Sports Network, August 23, 2017, https://bleacherreport.com/articles/2729018-the-definitive-history-of-trust-the-process.

that the Spirit is at work in a suffering believer's life, even if things look very messy right now.

4. If we've not experienced significant suffering, we may have difficulty identifying with someone's struggle. One man I know, a church leader who recently struggled with panic attacks, developed a newfound compassion for those in his congregation who were anxious and depressed. Earlier, he would have minimized their struggles and urged them to "believe the gospel," but over time he learned to listen and to bring more than generic truth from Scripture to bear on people's suffering. But even if you haven't experienced a specific struggle, you can grow in empathy as you listen closely and ask questions. We can take others' suffering seriously, even if we have not experienced the same kind and extent of suffering they have. We have all suffered in some way, and that should bring a sense of solidarity with fellow sufferers.

5. Perhaps we *have* experienced significant suffering, but we ourselves are wrestling with doubt about God's goodness to such an extent that our own faith is tenuous. This is a tricky one. It is hard to walk the path of faith with integrity without falling off to one of two sides: either the side of hollow assurances that don't measure up to the extent of suffering at hand, *or* the side of cynicism and doubt because the darkness has indeed appeared to overcome the light.

It's this latter barrier I'm focusing on now, the equivalent of being a spiritual 'Debbie Downer.'[3] While it is true that helpers are in process when it comes to spiritual growth as are counselees, significant and prolonged struggle in one or more areas may serve as a barrier in helping others, at least for a season. If

_____

3. A character created and played by Rachel Dratch on *Saturday Night Live*, whose negative mind-set and worst-case-scenario thinking dampened the spirits of everyone around her.

I'm wrestling with significant and prolonged cynicism, anger, doubt, and resentment in the midst of my own suffering, I will not be ready to offer the clarity and comfort necessary to help other strugglers. I need help myself, first and foremost. If you find yourself in this place, please go to other believers that you know and trust and ask them for prayer and counsel.

6. We're too focused on answering unanswerable questions. Suffering people generally aren't looking for tightly reasoned answers to theological and philosophical questions of God's goodness and the problem of evil. Those are important questions, of course, but they aren't usually front burner issues, particularly early on in ministry to someone. In addition, it's usually not helpful to speculate on God's purposes in permitting a particular form of suffering in a given person's life, as I mentioned earlier in "Ministry Priorities for Loving Sufferers."

7. We are fatigued and discouraged by facing the continual onslaught of suffering in our own lives and the lives of those we love. We find it hard to press into yet another person's pain. It's appropriate that helpers feel the weight of hardship as we come alongside fellow brothers or sisters as burden-bearers. Psychologist Diane Langberg says it pointedly:

> They bring you their stories. . . . They will take you to places you have never been and perhaps do not want to go. They will force you to be present to abuse, violence, death, deceit, brokenness and darkness. You sit surrounded by all of this stuff day after day, hour after hour, and you are an image bearer. You *will* be impacted or shaped.[4]

---

4. Diane Langberg, "The Spiritual Life of the Therapist: We Become What We Habitually Reflect," *Journal of Psychology and Christianity* 25, no. 3 (2006): 261.

Ministry indeed has a personal cost. Serving as an under-shepherd of the Good Shepherd Jesus is a weighty responsibility. We compound this weight by relying too much on our own strength and resources in ministry to the suffering. In the concluding chapter of this section, we'll focus on how it is ultimately the comfort of Christ we are bringing to others as we walk alongside those who are suffering.

Chapter 18

INCARNATING THE COMFORT OF CHRIST TO SUFFERERS

Ministry to those who are suffering is difficult. It often taxes our own faith and emotional strength to listen to stories of great affliction and misery, particularly in the midst of our own trials. How can we console others when we are so often in need of consolation ourselves? We do share in the sufferings of Christ, but the apostle Paul makes it clear that we also share in Christ's comfort. Paul's remarks in 2 Corinthians 1:3–7 help us in our own suffering and our ministry to others who are in the midst of hardship:

> Blessed be the God and Father of our Lord Jesus Christ, the Father of mercies and God of all comfort, who comforts us in all our affliction, so that we may be able to comfort those who are in any affliction, with the comfort with which we ourselves are comforted by God. For as we share abundantly in Christ's sufferings, so through

Christ we share abundantly in comfort too. If we are afflicted, it is for your comfort and salvation; and if we are comforted, it is for your comfort, which you experience when you patiently endure the same sufferings that we suffer. Our hope for you is unshaken, for we know that as you share in our sufferings, you will also share in our comfort.

There are two major themes here—the cascade effect Paul describes, and our union with Jesus Christ in his sufferings.[1]

The cascade effect is highlighted in verses 3–4, and repeated in verses 6–7. *The Father comforts us in our affliction so that we may comfort those in any affliction.* Comfort from the Father cascades down into our lives so that comfort may cascade from our lives into the lives of others who are suffering. Comfort flows downhill. We can ask four questions about this cascade: What is the source of the comfort? What is the endpoint? What kind of affliction? What kind of comfort? Let's look at each in order.

WHAT IS THE SOURCE OF THE COMFORT?

The source of the comfort is God, the "Father of mercies and God of all comfort." It's so easy for this phrase to roll off our tongues, but do we believe this? Do we bank on this in the midst of our own suffering or when we cry, "How long, O Lord?" on behalf of our suffering friends? There could be no waterfall of comfort cascading into our own lives if there were not endless headwaters of comfort in our God. Any other source will dry up. It's important to see that we are not generating the comfort,

---

1. Much of what follows in this chapter was originally given as a plenary address entitled, "Partners in Suffering and Comfort" at the CCEF National Conference, "Loss," held in San Diego, CA from October 3–5, 2014.

for ourselves or for others. We are acting as a reservoir and conduit for *God's* comfort. That's actually freeing—I personally do not have to be a source of inexhaustible comfort to someone—I can't be. The comfort buck doesn't start with me. But it doesn't stop with me either.

WHAT IS THE ENDPOINT?

The endpoint is the comfort of others. Suffering is meant ultimately to turn us outward rather than inward. Our own comfort, as important as it is, is not the end in itself. We are called to be a conduit and reservoir for the Father's comfort. It's important to recognize here that Paul doesn't have a time frame in mind for how quickly in the midst of our own suffering we experience the kind of comfort that enables us to move outward to others. That's especially important to hear if right now you're overwhelmed with your own losses. As I mentioned in the last chapter, you may be in a season of needing help before you can provide help.

While certainly one temptation in the midst of suffering is to become entrenched in a place of anguish and growing bitterness, immune from God's comfort and the comfort of others, there is also the opposite temptation to minimize the suffering we are experiencing. If this is the case we may try to move, bravely but perhaps prematurely, into ministry toward others. Do you ever feel that pressure, particularly if you are in vocational ministry, to minimize your losses and get on with the business of helping others? But do you see what this communicates to a fellow sufferer, even if you are not saying it explicitly? "What's wrong with you? You should be over this by now like I am."

Do you see the balance? The endpoint is a ministry of comfort to others, but the timetable for that endeavor will vary.

Reflecting on the process of coming to accept their child's disability, Stephanie Hubach writes, "rushed resolution results in resignation."[2] Similarly, the apostle Paul does not advocate stoic resignation. He is not saying, "Stuff your own difficulties so that you can focus on someone other than yourself." Just a few verses later in 2 Corinthians he says, "For we do not want you to be unaware, brothers, of the affliction we experienced in Asia. For we were so utterly burdened beyond our strength that we despaired of life itself" (1:8). He assumes and exemplifies in his own life that we participate in the ministry of comfort to others in the midst of our own hardships and growing pains.

Sarah exemplified this. She was a fellow collegiate team leader at a Navigators Ministries summer program during college. Sarah had been in a car accident and as a result had chronic, daily headaches. Every day began and ended with pounding in her head. She freely admitted how difficult this was for her, but also sought to entrust herself to a compassionate Father. The faithful wrestling with suffering and with her God that she had done to that point in time (and was still doing) paved the way for an incredible ministry among the participants of the program as they sought her out for care and counsel. She was wise beyond her years. As for me, my biggest trial to that point was failing a biochemistry exam, so I can't say people were seeking me out for my vast wisdom! But Sarah was a living example of the comfort cascade. Comfort flowed downhill from the Father of mercies into Sarah's life, and then, in time, it was multiplied into the lives of many struggling believers.

2. Stephanie Hubach, *Same Lake, Different Boat: Coming Alongside People Touched by Disability* (Phillipsburg, NJ: P & R, 2006), 110.

WHAT KIND OF AFFLICTION?

Now, what kind of affliction is Paul talking about? Is it only the affliction generated in the context of ministry? Is it only the suffering associated with persecution for the gospel? No, by virtue of the phrase, "so that we may be able to comfort those *who are in any affliction.*" Paul has in mind something broader than the suffering associated with living as a witness for Christ. Further, because it is God's comfort that we give, we don't have to experience the same exact suffering as someone else in order to provide comfort. I think this is one reason why Paul says it this way: we are comforted in *our* affliction so that we may comfort those in *any* affliction. I don't have to go through financial ruin to walk alongside someone who is experiencing that particular trial. Even if I haven't experienced disability in the aftermath of a stroke, I still can comfort someone who is in the midst of that suffering.

This should embolden us to move toward others who are suffering. We are setting before others Jesus Christ, first and foremost, not our own experiences, as consolation for hardships. No doubt, having a similar experience as another struggler is often helpful as a connecting point in ministry, but it is not a prerequisite for being a wise helper. In fact, there are times when it is a liability to project our particular experiences onto someone else's experience. Our own specific patterns of struggle (and what we found helpful) may or may not map onto others' lives.

WHAT KIND OF COMFORT?

What is the nature of the comfort we receive? This is an important question, because as we help others in the midst of their affliction, we are representing God's comfort to them. Because of this, learning to recognize the contours and characteristics of God's comfort is critical. Consider this question: What is the shape of God's comfort to you? What are you experiencing when you receive God's comfort? Perhaps it's easier to say what it is not. It's not a "there, there, it will be OK" kind of anemic assurance. And it's not simply a cognitive experience, an intellectual appreciation of who God is and what he's done. And it's not just an emotional experience either, like a bear hug from God. Clearly God's comfort is also not equated simply with relief or a reversal of fortunes, although it is wonderful when hard circumstances change. I sometimes miss God's comfort because I hold out for those things. So, what is the essence of God's comfort?

The essence of God's comfort is this: "I am here. I am with you. You are mine. You can trust me." And what is the token of that trust? The presence of the Holy Spirit, who Jesus describes as the Helper (Advocate or Counselor) in John 14:16. This is why Paul can say that the outcome of suffering is hope, "and hope does not put us to shame, because God's love has been poured into our hearts through the Holy Spirit who has been given to us" (Romans 5:5). And yet, comfort is not full and complete in this life because we do not see God face-to-face. Then, and only then, will all the sad things of life become untrue.[3] Until that time, we wait and cry out, "Come quickly, Lord Jesus." We bank our hope on God's presence with us now, and we extend his peace and presence to one another in word and deed ministry.

The second major thing to notice is that Jesus is central to the comfort cascade we experience. In verse 5 Paul highlights themes we looked at earlier regarding our union with Jesus Christ in his sufferings: "For as we share abundantly in Christ's

---

3. Author's paraphrase of Sam Gamgee's question to Gandalf in J.R.R. Tolkien, *The Return of the King: The Lord of the Rings, Part Three* (Boston: Houghton, Mifflin, Harcourt, 1994), 930.

sufferings, so through Christ we share abundantly in comfort too." Paul is reminding us that by his love, Jesus turns on the tap of the Father's comfort toward us. The gift of the Holy Spirit as the marker of God's comfort cannot happen apart from the life, death, resurrection, and ascension of Jesus Christ (John 16:7; Acts 2:33).

In his own sufferings, Jesus experienced God as the Father of mercies and God of all comfort. The Father matched abundant comfort to the abundant suffering in Jesus's life. What is true for Jesus is true for us. Affliction and comfort always travel as a pair. Our union with Christ in his suffering and comfort provides the living leverage so that our own sufferings can move us in an outward and others-oriented direction. We are partners with Christ in his suffering and comfort. This reality enables, motivates, and empowers us to be partners with others in their suffering.

So how can we know that the goal and endpoint of our suffering is comfort? Comfort that we experience and then extend to others who are struggling? Because the Father, Son, and Holy Spirit are intimately acquainted with the transformation of suffering into comfort. In our Father's infinite mercy, the cross is transformed into glory (1 Corinthians 1:18, 23–24; Hebrews 12:2). Notice that the dynamic Paul describes in 2 Corinthians 1:6 happens preeminently at the cross—*Jesus* was afflicted for our comfort and salvation. That most severe affliction became a fountain of living comfort, for himself and then for us.

If you are tempted to be cynical about this process of transforming suffering into comfort, in your own life or in others' lives, consider that God himself entered into that dynamic. He is with us, and he is for us. Although his purposes are mysterious, he is patiently and lovingly up to something good in the midst of our own cross-like sufferings. With this confidence, we serve as ambassadors of his comfort to others.

In summary, remember that God moves toward his suffering people with compassion and intentionality. We do the same in our everyday relationships and counseling ministry. Paul captures this ministry dynamic in 2 Corinthians 1:3–7 when he speaks of the way the comfort of Christ overflows into our lives so that we can minister comfort to others in the midst of their affliction. At the end of the day, we are offering more than ourselves to our suffering brothers and sisters in Christ; we are bringing the very comfort of Jesus Christ.

Wisely and tenderly coming alongside sufferers in their difficulty and sorrow is hard work. An equally challenging ministry is loving others in their struggle with sin. In the next part of the book, we turn our attention to the life-giving task of loving others who are caught in sin.

Part 4:
Loving Others as
Sinners

Chapter 19

SCRIPTURE SPEAKS TO SINNERS

The fact that I am a saint who sins confronted me from the very first moment I woke up yesterday. I hit the snooze button four times (after having plenty of sleep), ensuring that time in the Word and in prayer would be minimal at best. As I began my shower, already feeling angry with myself, I growled under my breath, "Grrr! Who left all this hair in the tub?" Worries about this particular day knotted my stomach as I sat down for breakfast. As I looked out the window and noticed a rain shower beginning, I complained inwardly, "Why do I have to walk the stupid dog every morning?" And that was just the first hour of the day! Can you identify with this?

The Heidelberg Catechism captures our human predicament succinctly in the phrase, "sin and misery." In the preceding section of the book we focused on misery (suffering). In this portion of the book, we will turn our attention to what it looks like to love people well who are struggling with sin.

Being attentive to where God is at work in a person's life (approaching them as saints) and knowing people well enough to feel the weight of their suffering (approaching them as sufferers) builds gospel-saturated relationships. But if the extent of our one-another ministry is affirmation and consolation, then (as important as those ministry priorities are) we are missing a critical aspect of loving others well. Scripture clearly portrays the origin of humanity's problems as sin (Genesis 3). Adam and Eve mistrusted the goodness of God, their Creator. They wanted to be like God and they disobeyed his command, sending all of creation into a literal death spiral. Like a massive nuclear blast with shock waves spreading out across the globe, our first parents' rebellion set in motion all that was and is wrong with our world and our relationships with God and others. In that sense, sin is our deepest problem as human beings.

SIN IS AN EVER-PRESENT REALITY

Every single person must reckon with the fact that "none is righteous, no not one; no one understands; no one seeks for God. All have turned aside; together they have become worthless; no one does good, not even one" (Romans 3:10–12). "All have sinned and fall short of the glory of God" (Romans 3:23). We know this experientially as well. We are not only victims of sin (sufferers); we are also perpetrators of wrongdoing (sinners). We are harmed and we harm others. Repeatedly.

God is holy and loving and he cannot turn a blind eye toward sin. Thankfully, he has acted decisively and redemptively through his Son Jesus Christ's death and resurrection to forgive our sin and cleanse us from unrighteousness (Titus 3:3–7; 1 John 1:9). In Jesus, believers are justified and reconciled to God (Romans 5:6–11). Our heart of stone is changed to a heart of flesh (Ezekiel 36:26). While still dead in our sins, God makes us alive in Christ (Ephesians 2:5). And then he says to his people, "Be holy, for I am holy" (Leviticus 11:45b, quoted in 1 Peter 1:16).

It's an understatement to say that we find it difficult to live holy lives! Sin is an ever-present reality. Consider just your last week. Where have your thoughts, attitudes, motives, words, and actions been inconsistent with God's Word? Where have the "works of the flesh" (Galatians 5:19–21) manifested more evidently than the "fruit of the Spirit" (Galatians 5:22–23)? Over the last week I noticed impatience, passivity, fear of man, judgmental thoughts, anger, avoidance of conflict, love of comfort, self-pity, and envy, among other things in my life. And I noticed others doing some of those same things—both friends and strangers.

The Confession of Sin from *The Book of Common Prayer* captures well the totality of our experience with unruly desires and actions:

> Almighty and most merciful Father,
> we have erred and strayed from your ways like lost sheep.
> We have followed too much the devices and desires
> of our own hearts.
> We have offended against your holy laws.
> We have left undone those things which we ought to have done,
> and we have done those things which we ought not
> to have done;
> and apart from your grace, there is no health in us.
> O Lord, have mercy upon us.
> Spare all those who confess their faults.
> Restore all those who are penitent, according to your promises
> declared to all people in Christ Jesus our Lord.
> And grant, O most merciful Father, for his sake,
> that we may now live a godly, righteous, and sober life,
> to the glory of your holy Name. Amen.[1]

1. Anglican Church in North America, *The Book of Common Prayer*

Our own experience of sin as God's people is not unique. As I first discussed in *Cross Talk*, the Bible presupposes that we are faced incessantly with evils from *within* ourselves. Sin's pervasive reality is like gravity; it continually pulls the people of God downward.[2] In the Old Testament, the people of Israel struggled with sin despite having been redeemed from their slavery and brought into covenant relationship with the Lord. God gave them the Ten Commandments to order their steps in keeping with his design for humanity to image him faithfully (Exodus 20:1–17; Deuteronomy 5:1–22). But Torah (Law) was not enough. Animal sacrifices for sin could not ultimately atone for sin (Hebrews 10:4, 11). Apart from a spiritual heart transplant and the gift of the Spirit (Ezekiel 36:25–27) bestowed through the atoning sacrifice of Jesus Christ (Hebrews 10:12–14), there is no hope for sinners. Like the apostle Paul, we cry out, "Who will deliver me from this body of death?" (Romans 7:24). And we answer with him, "Thanks be to God through Jesus Christ our Lord!" (Romans 7:25).

SAINTS STILL STRUGGLE WITH SIN

But new life in Christ is by no means automatic, as though the gift of the Spirit confers instantaneous, experiential perfection. We are saints, but saints who struggle with the ongoing presence of sin. Even though the power of sin has been broken and the penalty for sin has been paid for us in Jesus Christ, continued wrestling with sin—war between flesh and Spirit—characterizes our lives in the time between Jesus's resurrection and his return. We find that, as the old hymn says, we are "prone to wander . . . prone to leave the God [we] love."[3] That's why the New Testament epistles are so

(Huntington Beach, CA: Anglican Liturgy Press, 2019), 12.

2. Emlet, *Cross Talk*, 77.

3. "Come Thou Fount of Every Blessing," Hymn #457, *Trinity Hymnal*,

full of instruction, exhortation, correction, and warning for God's people. We still battle the world, the flesh (our own inner desires for something besides God), and the devil as we seek to love God and neighbor (Matthew 22:34–40).

We need the ongoing grace and mercy of Jesus through his Spirit to transform us bit-by-bit into his character. What a noble end to our journey as believers that we should be like God (1 Corinthians 2:9; 2 Peter 1:4; 1 John 3:2)! This hope undergirds our daily battle for purity of life (1 John 3:3). Coming alongside fellow believers in this battle is crucial. Personal holiness is not simply an individual event but a corporate effort, accomplished in the context of relationships and worship in the local church (Ecclesiastes 4:9–12; Galatians 6:1–2; Hebrews 10:24–25).

Affirming that sin is our deepest problem is different than saying, "Sin is all we talk about." Or, "Sin is always the first thing we talk about." At the same time, full-orbed one-another ministry must address the ways in which we who are saints of God still live contrary to God's design. Ultimately, it's not loving to persistently overlook a brother's or sister's sin. The question is, how do we challenge patterns of sin and call someone to obedience in winsome ways?

OUR REDEEMED IDENTITY IS THE BASIS FOR OBEDIENCE

As always, God, in his Word, is our best guide for how to effectively and lovingly deal with sin. As we read Scripture as a whole, we find an overall pattern to the way God appeals to his people for their obedience. This pattern has sometimes been called the pairing of the "indicative" and the "imperative." God declares/reminds his people who they are by virtue of his redemptive action (indicative) and then he calls them to obey in

revised ed. (Atlanta, GA: Great Commission Publications, 1990).

keeping with their new identity (imperative). Put another way, relationship precedes (and generates) rules. Calling precedes (and generates) commands. We "do" because God has "done." God tells his people repeatedly, "I have made you my own. Now live in keeping with your identity as my covenant people." Or to use the framework and language of this book, "Because you are saints, seek to root out everything in your life that doesn't match who you are as a child of God."

At baseline then, addressing sin in believers' lives builds on the foundation of God's prior, personal, and powerful redeeming work. Here are just a few places in Scripture where you see this indicative and imperative connection:

- "I am the LORD your God, who brought you out of the land of Egypt, out of the house of slavery [indicative]. You shall have no other gods before me" [imperative] (Exodus 20:2–3).

- "Let not sin therefore reign in your mortal body, to make you obey its passions [imperative]. Do not present your members to sin as instruments for unrighteousness [imperative], but present yourselves to God [imperative] as those who have been brought from death to life [indicative], and your members to God as instruments for righteousness" [imperative] (Romans 6:12–13).

- "If then you have been raised with Christ [indicative], seek the things that are above [imperative], where Christ is, seated at the right hand of God [indicative]. Set your minds on things that are above, not on things that are on earth [imperative]. For you have died, and your life is hidden with Christ in God [indicative]. When Christ who is your life appears, then you also will appear with him in glory [indicative]. Put to death therefore what is earthly in you: sexual immorality, impurity, passion, evil desire, and covetousness, which is idolatry" [imperative] (Colossians 3:1–5).

In each of these passages, God appeals to his people's redeemed identity as the basis for their repentance and/or obedience. And as we saw in Part Two of this book, the very fact that the apostle Paul refers to the problem-riddled Corinthians as "saints" who will be blameless on the day of the Lord (1 Corinthians 1:2, 8) provides the foundation to directly challenge the ways they have been living contrary to their identity in Christ.

As we now consider several places in Scripture where sin and obedience are explicitly addressed, we need to remember that the indicative is always at least implicit for believers, who are the primary audience of the Bible. The call to obedience is always embedded in God's redemptive, identity-shifting work, even if the biblical writer is not highlighting it in the moment.

What does this mean for addressing sin in the lives of unbelievers who have not embraced by faith the good news of Jesus Christ? It means that our counsel will reference Jesus Christ's life-giving and heart-changing work as the basis for change. (That's true for believers as well, of course!) We are not looking for self-initiated and self-directed change in behavior, but a total renovation of the soul from the inside out, which is ultimately God's effectual work (Ephesians 2:8–9). This doesn't mean that every conversation with non-Christians is explicitly evangelistic, but it does mean that as we walk alongside struggling unbelievers we situate their lives in the bigger story of Scripture, pointing them toward the hope of Jesus Christ. We yearn for them to get to the point of confessing, "apart from you, Jesus, I can do nothing" (John 15:5).

THE CALL TO REPENTANCE FOR BELIEVERS AND UNBELIEVERS

Repentance is a change of direction in our lives, a turning from our sinful desires and actions and a turning to Christ for the forgiveness of our particular sins and the grace necessary to walk in obedience. A call to repentance for believers grows out of their identity as God's people and the confidence that God will finish what he has begun (Philippians 1:6). A call to repentance for unbelievers will appeal to their inherent worth as God's image bearers, fallen as they are, and urge them to embrace by faith, God's remedy for their sinful condition—the forgiveness and righteousness offered through Jesus Christ's atoning work on the Cross and his resurrection from the dead. However, the specific contours of lovingly probing patterns of sin and calling others to obedience described in the next chapters will show significant overlap between believers and unbelievers.

The dynamics and outworking of the desires of the heart in the genesis of sin are similar in both regenerate and unregenerate people, although their standing before God and their relationship to the sin nature is radically different because of the work of the Spirit in giving new birth to those he calls. Further, what God has done in Jesus Christ always undergirds a call to repentance and obedience, whether a person is responding for the first time (unbeliever) or for the hundredth time (believer). Faith in what Jesus has done (indicative) precedes acting on it (imperative) for both unbelievers and believers. Thus, there is a common thread in ministry methodology to believers and unbelievers alike: indicatives to believe/trust precede imperatives to follow.

Given this backdrop of how the call to turn from sin and to pursue obedience rests on the redemptive, identity-shifting work of Jesus Christ, in the next chapter we will get more specific about how addressing sin might look in interpersonal ministry by examining several biblical examples.

Chapter 20

HOW GOD LOVES SINNERS: BIBLICAL EXAMPLES

How does God love people as sinners? How are the wayward approached? How are rebellious people wooed to repentance and its refreshing fruits? Again, there are many places in Scripture (almost every page!) where we witness God moving *toward* his people even as he moves *against* their sin. But let's focus primarily on Jesus himself, especially because we can see clearly the variation in the way he handles the sin of those he ministers to. He is a master of contextualization, attentive to the details of the person in front of him. Let's look briefly at three snapshots of ministry in Jesus's life—his encounters with the Samaritan woman, the rich young ruler, and the Pharisees.

In these cases, Jesus is addressing sin issues in those who have not yet professed faith in him. Nonetheless, I believe there is much to learn from these encounters for the way we address sin in the lives of believers, given the overlap in ministry approach between those who have already put their faith in Christ and those who have not.

1. *The Samaritan woman* (John 4). We'll focus on the moment when Jesus gets to the heart of this woman's life. Jesus has been talking to her about the living water that he gives, but she is still thinking in physical terms. We pick up the action in verses 15–18:

> The woman said to him, "Sir, give me this water, so that I will not be thirsty or have to come here to draw water." Jesus said to her, "Go, call your husband, and come here." The woman answered him, "I have no husband." Jesus said to her, "You are right in saying, 'I have no husband'; for you have had five husbands, and the one you now have is not your husband. What you have said is true."

Notice that Jesus says things that put the issue of obedience to God on the table: "Go, call your husband." And he uses the woman's own words to further that aim by revealing her sin: "You're right. The fact is, you have had five husbands and the man you're with now is not your husband." Busted! But in the most winsome way.

The woman doesn't miss a beat:

> The woman said to him, "Sir, I perceive that you are a prophet. Our fathers worshiped on this mountain, but you say that in Jerusalem is the place where people ought to worship." Jesus said to her, "Woman, believe me, the hour is coming when neither on this mountain nor in Jerusalem will you worship the Father. You worship what you do not know; we worship what we know, for salvation is from the Jews. But the hour is

coming, and is now here, when the true worshipers will worship the Father in spirit and truth, for the Father is seeking such people to worship him. God is spirit, and those who worship him must worship in spirit and truth." The woman said to him, "I know that Messiah is coming (he who is called Christ). When he comes, he will tell us all things." Jesus said to her, "I who speak to you am he" (vv. 19–26).

As a result of this revelation of her sin and of Jesus's identity, the woman is moved to action. She runs back to her village and says, "Come, see a man who told me all that I ever did" (John 4:29). Normally that level of exposure in our lives makes us want to run and hide. Why was she not crippled by guilt and shame? Jesus had already (against all social norms) reached into her world. He demonstrated that her ethnicity and gender were not barriers to his love. She must have sensed also in Jesus's words the message that God does not reveal what he does not intend to heal. She must have experienced Jesus saying, "Neither do I condemn you; go, and from now on sin no more" (see John 8:11). As a result, not only she, but many Samaritans believed.

2. *The rich young ruler* (Mark 10:17–24). We now come to a briefer interchange, but one that is instructive also—Jesus's interaction with the rich young ruler:

And as he was setting out on his journey, a man ran up and knelt before him and asked him, "Good Teacher, what must I do to inherit eternal life?" And Jesus said to him, "Why do you call me good? No one is good except God alone. You know the commandments: 'Do not murder, Do not commit adultery, Do not steal, Do not bear false witness, Do not defraud, Honor your father and mother.'" And he said to him, "Teacher, all these I have kept from my youth." And Jesus, looking at him, loved him, and said to him, "You lack one thing: go, sell all that you have and give to the poor, and you will have treasure in heaven; and come, follow me." Disheartened by the saying, he went away sorrowful, for he had great possessions. And Jesus looked around and said to his disciples, "How difficult it will be for those who have wealth to enter the kingdom of God!" And the disciples were amazed at his words. But Jesus said to them again, "Children, how difficult it is to enter the kingdom of God!"

What do we notice here? Jesus looked at him and loved him. This shows the dignity Jesus afforded those he spoke with. His underlying posture toward this image bearer and seeker was love. Jesus then moved toward the heart, in a way similar to what he said in Matthew 6:21, "For where your treasure is, there your heart will be also." The young man's treasure—and his heart—were bound up in his riches. Jesus loved him enough to reveal his heart. He graciously revealed sins of omission, not only sins of commission. And the man had a choice to make, an action to consider.

Now, if these were the only kind of interactions we saw Jesus having we might be tempted to think, "Don't confront directly. Always go in the back door when you are challenging someone on his or her sin." But then we read about Jesus's encounters with the Pharisees.

3. *The Pharisees* (Matthew 23:27–28). The Gospels record many interactions between Jesus and the Pharisees, but we'll look at a portion of the "seven woes" Jesus levels against the scribes and Pharisees in Matthew 23:

"Woe to you, scribes and Pharisees, hypocrites! For you are like whitewashed tombs, which outwardly appear beautiful, but within are full of dead people's bones and all uncleanness. So you also outwardly appear righteous to others, but within you are full of hypocrisy and lawlessness."

Notice that Jesus was toughest on the hard-hearted, blind, and consistently self-righteous religious leaders. This is in line with Old Testament prophetic denunciation of shepherds (leaders) who were oppressing their flock (the people of Israel). Ezekiel 34:4 is characteristic: "The weak you have not strengthened, the sick you have not healed, the injured you have not bound up, the strayed you have not brought back, the lost you have not sought, and with force and harshness you have ruled them." The same was true of the religious leaders of Jesus's day, and he calls them out directly and to their faces.

These snapshots from Jesus's ministry provide our starting point to examine in greater detail how we might love sinners well.

Chapter 21

MINISTRY PRIORITIES FOR LOVING SINNERS

We encounter multiple opportunities each week to move toward fellow sinners. Here are just a few situations you may have experienced recently:

- You learn that instead of going to youth group, your daughter spent the evening with several non-Christian friends. You know this because you encountered them at the mall where you were shopping.
- You see that your roommate's critical and judgmental spirit is impacting the members of the small group you lead. People are reluctant to speak during the Bible study discussion, and some have stopped coming altogether.
- The husband of the couple you are counseling consistently fails to demonstrate concern and practical care for his wife who is struggling physically in the last months of

her pregnancy. His wife feels neglected, discouraged, and overwhelmed.

While ministry to each person—daughter, friend, and husband—will vary, taking into account the specifics of each situation, what are the commonalities of a wise approach? Building from the biblical examples discussed in the preceding chapter, let's explore some implications for the way we love others by challenging their sin.

ENGAGE THE HEART

We should exhibit winsome, heart-oriented engagement. In all three examples, Jesus goes deeper than dealing with behavior, as important as that is. Jesus speaks explicitly about the centrality of the heart in Luke 6:43–45:

> "For no good tree bears bad fruit, nor again does a bad tree bear good fruit, for each tree is known by its own fruit. For figs are not gathered from thornbushes, nor are grapes picked from a bramble bush. The good person out of the good treasure of his heart produces good, and the evil person out of his evil treasure produces evil, for out of the abundance of the heart his mouth speaks."

Similarly, in Matthew 15:17–19, Jesus says:

> "Do you not see that whatever goes into the mouth passes into the stomach and is expelled? But what comes out of the mouth proceeds from the heart, and this defiles a person. For out of the heart come evil thoughts, murder, adultery, sexual immorality, theft, false witness, slander."

Sin flows from the heart. This biblical focus on the heart, our moral center and source of motivation, reminds us that all of life is lived before God. Humans can't escape their image-bearing status. We worship either the Creator or created things, moment by moment (Romans 1:25). In that sense, sin is disordered worship. "Why do I do what I do?" is closely aligned with the question "To whom or what is my heart most directed right now?"

In light of this, you will want to ask questions of people that get to the desires and fears that are at the root of all sin. In what specific ways is your friend, child, or counselee drawn to loves other than Jesus Christ and his kingdom? What do they want, crave, value, cherish, fear, trust, treasure, seek refuge in, or serve more than the living God?[1]

Recently, I started counseling someone who struggles with alcohol abuse. I asked him questions about all facets of his life—upbringing, family, work, church—in order to get a feel for the pressure points in his life, as well as the places of joy. My assignment for him after that first session was to reflect on the thoughts, desires, and fears that were associated with the temptation to drink. He thanked me for not simply making that first session about behavioral strategies to help him stop drinking. Most everyone else in his life was simply saying, "Stop it!" Was I concerned about his drinking? Absolutely. But it was a ministry priority to help him uncover the *whys* of his drinking binges.

That's what James is highlighting when he asks, "What causes quarrels and what causes fights among you?" (4:1a). He doesn't answer, "It's because this other person is mean and argumentative." Or, "Because you had a bad night's sleep." As

---

1. For an expanded discussion, see David Powlison, "X-ray Questions: Drawing Out the Whys and Wherefores of Human Behavior," *The Journal of Biblical Counseling* 18, no. 1 (1999): 2–9; and Edward T. Welch, *Motives: "Why Do I Do the Things I Do?"* (Phillipsburg, NJ: P & R, 2003).

important as these interpersonal and contextual matters are (for examples, see Proverbs 15:1 and Ephesians 6:4), Scripture emphasizes our agency and responsibility in matters of sin and righteousness. In keeping with this emphasis, James answers his own question, "Is it not this, that your passions are at war within you? You desire and do not have, so you murder. You covet and cannot obtain, so you fight and quarrel" (4:1b–2a).

In light of this, Proverbs 20:5 describes our task as intentional friends and counselors: "The purpose in a man's heart is like deep water, but a man of understanding will draw it out." We seek to engage at the level of heart motives and desires. We help people see how they are forsaking "the fountain of living waters" and are digging "broken cisterns that can hold no water" (Jeremiah 2:13). We pray that the wonder, beauty, and glory of God's character and redemptive work revealed in Scripture will transform affections and motivate a change in behavior.[2]

BE MOTIVATED BY LOVE

Love must be the motive in our ministry to sinners. This is implicit in all Jesus's interactions, but it is explicit in his encounter with the rich young ruler. Too often I find—for example, in my correction of sin in my children—that I'm more concerned about my own comfort, peace, and control than their spiritual wellbeing. Growling, "Who left all these dirty dishes in the sink?" does not communicate, "I love you" by its tone, even if the issue needs to be addressed. But if love is my motive, more likely I will be direct and winsome. Further, with love as the motive, we are more empowered to fight against our people-pleasing and fear

---

2. For more on this dynamic, see the sermon by Thomas Chalmers, "The Expulsive Power of a New Affection." The full text is available at https://www.monergism.com/thethreshold/sdg/Chalmers,%20Thomas%20-%20The%20Exlpulsive%20Power%20of%20a%20New%20Af.pdf.

of conflict, which might lead to silence when a timely word of warning is necessary.

Throughout Scripture, even when God is denouncing sin through his prophets or apostles, love, mercy, and compassion form the backbone of his appeal. Listen to God's heart, first in these Old Testament passages:

> But Zion said, "The Lord has forsaken me;
>   my Lord has forgotten me."
> "Can a woman forget her nursing child,
>   that she should have no compassion on the son of her womb?
> Even these may forget,
>   yet I will not forget you.
> Behold, I have engraved you on the palms of my hands;
>   your walls are continually before me." (Isaiah 49:14–16)

> Go, and proclaim these words toward the north, and say,
> "'Return, faithless Israel,
> declares the Lord.
> I will not look on you in anger,
>   for I am merciful,
> declares the Lord;
> I will not be angry forever.
> Only acknowledge your guilt,
>   that you rebelled against the Lord your God
> and scattered your favors among foreigners under every green tree,
>   and that you have not obeyed my voice,
> declares the Lord.'" (Jeremiah 3:12–13)

"'I said,
　How I would set you among my sons,
and give you a pleasant land,
　a heritage most beautiful of all nations.
And I thought you would call me, My Father,
　and would not turn from following me
Surely, as a treacherous wife leaves her husband,
　so have you been treacherous to me, O house of Israel,
declares the Lord.'" (Jeremiah 3:19–20)

When Israel was a child, I loved him,
　and out of Egypt I called my son.
The more they were called,
　the more they went away;
they kept sacrificing to the Baals
　and burning offerings to idols.
Yet it was I who taught Ephraim to walk;
　I took them up by their arms,
　but they did not know that I healed them.
I led them with cords of kindness,
　with the bands of love,
and I became to them as one who eases the yoke on their jaws,
　and I bent down to them and fed them. (Hosea 11:1–4)

How can I give you up, O Ephraim?
　How can I hand you over, O Israel?
How can I make you like Admah?
　How can I treat you like Zeboiim?
My heart recoils within me;
　my compassion grows warm and tender.

I will not execute my burning anger;
  I will not again destroy Ephraim;
for I am God and not a man,
  the Holy One in your midst,
  and I will not come in wrath. (Hosea 11:8–9)

The LORD your God is in your midst,
  a mighty one who will save;
he will rejoice over you with gladness;
  he will quiet you by his love;
he will exult over you with loud singing. (Zephaniah 3:17)

This is just a small sample of the multiple passages in the Old Testament that condemn sin and call God's people to repentance. As you read, can you see how the burning love of God drives his appeal and ultimately leads to his own arm working salvation and restoration for his people (Isaiah 59:16)?

We observe the same juxtaposition of a merciful love and a clear-eyed stance against sin in the New Testament epistles. Listen to Paul's heart for God's people in the context of his letters in which he boldly addresses problems in each church:

But God shows his love for us in that while we were still sinners, Christ died for us. (Romans 5:8)

I do not write these things to make you ashamed, but to admonish you as my beloved children. For though you have countless guides in Christ, you do not have many fathers. For I became your father in Christ Jesus through the gospel. (1 Corinthians 4:14–15)

We have spoken freely to you, Corinthians, and opened wide our hearts to you. We are not withholding our affection from you, but you are withholding yours from us. As a fair exchange—I speak as to my children—open wide your hearts also. (2 Corinthians 6:11–13, NIV)

My little children . . . I am again in the anguish of childbirth until Christ is formed in you! (Galatians 4:19)

Brothers, if anyone is caught in any transgression, you who are spiritual should restore him in a spirit of gentleness. (Galatians 6:1a)

But we were gentle among you, like a nursing mother taking care of her own children. So, being affectionately desirous of you, we were ready to share with you not only the gospel of God but also our own selves, because you had become very dear to us. (1 Thessalonians 2:7–8)

For you know how, like a father with his children, we exhorted each one of you and encouraged you and charged you to walk in a manner worthy of God, who calls you into his own kingdom and glory. (1 Thessalonians 2:11–12)

In both the Old and New Testament, a clarion call for God's people to live holy lives is always undergirded and motivated by the relational bond of love that exists between God and his people. God is a lover who is jealous for his wayward wife to return to a marriage in which she is meant to thrive. We are called to incarnate God's heart in interpersonal ministry. Love communicates, "I'm passionate about you flourishing as a human being in the way God intended you to. I care too much about you to let you settle for cheap substitutes that promise and never ultimately deliver those goods."

LOOK FOR AND EXPECT REPENTANCE

Always expect and hope for repentance. No one is a hopeless case. Who would have thought that, given her history, the Samaritan woman would repent? Pray and anticipate that the Spirit will move in the other person's life, whether believer or unbeliever. Even from among the Pharisees, Jesus had true seekers and converts. Think of Nicodemus. Or the apostle Paul, who had been intent on destroying the church and self-identified as the chief of sinners (1 Timothy 1:15). And for the believers in Thessalonica, Paul expresses this confidence:

> Now may the God of peace himself sanctify you completely, and may your whole spirit and soul and body be kept blameless at the coming of our Lord Jesus Christ. He who calls you is faithful; he will surely do it. (1 Thessalonians 5:23–24)

Confidence in the Spirit's work grounds our hope for obedience in the lives of those we love and counsel. This does not mean that we are naïve when it comes to entrenched and destructive sin patterns, including abuse and addictions. True repentance is demonstrated by "a long obedience in the same direction," to use Eugene Peterson's phrase.[3]

Finally, even when a professing believer persistently refuses to repent, a hope for restoration undergirds the administration of church discipline. Even the radical step of excommunication has the end in mind of a wayward person returning to Christ (1 Corinthians 5:4–5; 1 Timothy 1:20).

---

3. Eugene Peterson, *A Long Obedience in the Same Direction: Discipleship in an Instant Society, Commemorative Edition* (Downers Grove, IL: IVP, 2019).

RELATIONSHIP IS THE BASIS FOR SHARING CONCERNS

Build on the foundation of your relational standing with the person.
This is implicit in Jesus's standing as a rabbi in his culture. He had the right to speak in all three of these situations. (Of course, he also had authority as the Son of God.) What about for us? Generally, the better I know someone and the more they trust me, the greater freedom I have to speak more challenging words into their lives.

I met with a couple yesterday I have known for many years and have counseled during various seasons of struggle. Over the most recent months of working with them, their relationship has deteriorated into entrenched patterns of self-protection. Neither wants to do the consistently hard work of laying down their lives for the other, trusting that God will indeed provide the grace and mercy they need to persevere and thrive. Their fears of a doomed and hopeless marriage are becoming a self-fulfilling prophecy. They appreciated my forthright assessment and call to honor Christ by looking not only to their own interests but also to the interests of the other (Philippians 2:4). At the same time, I needed to be careful I didn't presume on that relational trust and become sloppy and sinful in my approach; it's too easy to abuse position and authority. For example, if I had exhibited an irritated, impatient, or exasperated tone as I spoke with them, I would not have stewarded well our friendship and the opportunity to speak life-giving words to them.

CHALLENGE WITH A POSTURE OF HUMILITY AND MERCY

Exhibit a posture of humility and mercy. This is especially evident in Jesus's prolonged and thoughtful engagement with the Samaritan woman. She had three strikes against her in a first-century

Jewish context: she came from an "unclean" culture, she was a woman, and she was actively living in sin. Did that deter Jesus? No. Consider how the writer of Hebrews describes Jesus: "For we do not have a high priest who is unable to sympathize with our weaknesses, but one who in every respect has been tempted as we are, yet without sin" (Hebrews 4:15). If Jesus, the perfect Son of God, fully identifies and empathizes with us no matter where we come from and no matter what we have done, what does that mean for all of us who are far from perfect in the way we relate to fellow sinners?

If our basic posture toward people is one of mercy, and if people see *us* being humble and honest about our own sin, then when we correct others, it will feel like a caring act of love to them. Consider what Galatians 6:1–2 says:

> Brothers, if anyone is caught in any transgression, you who are spiritual should restore him in a spirit of gentleness. Keep watch on yourself, lest you too be tempted. Bear one another's burdens, and so fulfill the law of Christ.

Restoration, not judgment, is in view. Helping someone overcome his or her sin is a rescue mission. It is bearing another person's burdens, not making them heavier with a sense of condemnation and shame. Having our own hearts in the right place is key. Humility and gentleness go hand in hand.

REPENTANCE MEANS PUTTING OFF AND PUTTING ON

Urge repentance that is associated with clear steps of obedience. Jesus's call to the rich young ruler to sell his belongings and follow Jesus demonstrates this reality. Honestly facing sin involves more than simply agreeing that what you're doing is wrong. It is more than understanding situational triggers and temptations for sin. And it is more than possessing insight into the heart motivations beneath the particular sin. Rather, repentance and faith—actually turning *from* sin and turning *to* Christ in trust and dependence—is a necessary and ongoing dynamic of the Christian life. Holy Spirit wrought insight, conviction, and empowerment should lead to actions consistent with God's revealed will in Scripture. In light of God's saving work for us and in us, our lives should be marked by a struggle for increasing conformity to the character of Jesus. "Not that I have already obtained this or am already perfect, but I press on to make it my own, because Christ Jesus has made me his own" (Philippians 3:12).

Paul captures the progressive and ongoing change dynamic this way: "Finally, then, brothers, we ask and urge you in the Lord Jesus, that as you received from us how you ought to walk and to please God, just as you are doing, that you do so more and more" (1 Thessalonians 4:1). More particularly, Paul urges the Ephesians to:

> Put off your old self, which belongs to your former manner of life and is corrupt through deceitful desires, and to be renewed in the spirit of your minds, and to put on the new self, created after the likeness of God in true righteousness and holiness. (Ephesians 4:22–24)

He expands on this put off/put on dynamic in the verses that follow. Put away falsehood and put on speaking the truth (4:25). Put off stealing and put on honest labor (4:28). Put off corrupting talk and put on speech that builds up and gives grace to hearers (4:29). Put away bitterness, anger, and slander and put on kindness, tenderheartedness, and forgiveness (4:31– 32). No wonder Martin Luther said that "the entire life of believers [was] to be one of repentance."[4] We are to progressively "grow up in every way into him who is the head, into Christ" (Ephesians 4:15), while at the same time embracing the mercy and forgiveness of Jesus for our inevitable failures (Psalm 32:5; Proverbs 28:13; 1 John 1:9).

As I close out this chapter on ministry priorities for loving people as sinners, I want to make a few final comments. First, I find that when counseling Christians in a more formal setting, people often come in already aware of and grieved over their sins. They are actively seeking help. My task is usually less about confrontation and more about helping them understand the desires and fears that underlie their sinful behaviors and urging them toward practical steps of love toward God and others. In a church or more informal ministry setting, you will do this heart-probing work too, but you will likely encounter more occasions in which people are less receptive to your counsel because they don't yet see what you and others have observed.

Second—and this you see in Jesus's encounter with the Pharisees—when sin oppresses or threatens the safety of others, we need to intervene very quickly, directly and forthrightly. Situations of domestic violence or out-of-control substance abuse would be examples that I mentioned earlier in the book. Also, while we hope and pray for repentance with regard to abusers, assessing the genuineness of their contrition in the moment is not always easy. They need to bear fruit in keeping with repentance (Matthew 3:8) over time, consistently putting off entitlement, anger, harshness, and control—and putting on humility, gentleness, mercy, and love.

Third, ministry to sinners is a long-term commitment. Very rarely, if ever, will we have a Nathan and David moment (2 Samuel 12:1–15), in which we skillfully lead a sin-blinded

---

4. Martin Luther, "The 95 Theses," KDG Wittenberg, https://www.luther.de/en/95thesen.html.

friend or counselee to a place of maximum vulnerability and then say, "You are the man [or woman]!" and the person responds, "I have sinned." Oh, if it were only that easy! Most of the time I find that addressing sin in others' lives is similar to what I experience in my own life—a gradual peeling away of multiple layers of behavior, thoughts, attitudes, affections, and motives that diverge from God's good plan for me.

A wonderful literary picture of this process is found in C. S. Lewis's *The Voyage of the Dawn Treader*, when Aslan peels layers of dragon skin from Eustace, restoring and redeeming him to his true humanity.[5] This also reminds us that the process of purification in our lives is often quite painful. Two steps forward and one step back is often the pattern of change. Micro-steps rather than huge leaps forward most often characterize our fight against sin. In light of this reality, are we as patient in loving others through the messy process of change as God is with us?

Fourth, confronting sin directly is not the only path to repentance. Don't forget that God's kindness can and does have the same effect. Paul highlights this in Romans 2:4 by saying, "Or do you presume on the riches of his kindness and forbearance and patience, not knowing that God's kindness is meant to lead you to repentance?" His kindness softens our hearts. This is true in relation to others as well. There have been times when I expected a "stick" in response to my wrongdoing, but instead was a given the equivalent of a "carrot" from the offended party (i.e., a gracious and forgiving posture). Being a recipient of mercy (and not only justice) deepens my motivation to do everything possible to bring healing and reconciliation to the relationship.

---

5. C. S. Lewis, *The Voyage of the Dawn Treader*, The Chronicles of Narnia, Book 5 (New York: HarperCollins, 1980), 106–11.

Chapter 22

HOW WE LOVE SINNERS: EVERYDAY EXAMPLES

How does the biblical call to address sin look in everyday ministry? Let's start with family, since that is a prime place for us to notice and respond to others' sins. At this point my daughter is twenty and my son is eighteen. Addressing sin in their lives now looks different than when they were five and three, although the same ministry priorities hold true. Now there is the opportunity to engage them more deeply and expansively.

I have found that how I approach them every day impacts how they receive my input about their sins. If I have a track record of pointing out the good work of God in their lives, they are generally more receptive to inquiry and possible correction—the pairing of indicative and imperative in action. Consistently approaching them as a saint sets the stage for approaching them as a sinner. It is helpful when I preface the conversation by saying, "Could I talk with you about something I've noticed over the last few days?" I try to do something similar in a counseling setting. For example, "Could we talk about something I've noticed over our last two sessions regarding how you speak about your wife?" Even better is to use the counselee's own words to gain entrée into a discussion of sinful attitudes and behavior: "You mentioned a few minutes ago that you feel your heart hardening toward your daughter. Could we back up and talk about that more fully?"

TONE IS KEY

If I communicate irritation or impatience from the start, it's likely not to go well. This is why examining our own hearts and praying for a posture of humility and the motive of love is critical to serving as a faithful mirror to our friends' and counselees' sinful patterns. Are you addressing sin because you deeply love this person and want him or her to flourish in keeping with God's design? Or is your confrontation a knee-jerk, self-protective, fear-based, or comfort-driven intervention? I find that if I am more "mad than sad" about my children's sin, I have my own heart issues of pride, self-righteousness, control, and performance to address first before God, as a prerequisite to approaching them in humility. This doesn't mean that anger over sin is inappropriate. It's just that, unlike God, our anger so quickly morphs from righteous to unrighteous. This is why James 1:19–20 says, "Know this, my beloved brothers: let every person be quick to hear, slow to speak, slow to anger; for the anger of man does not produce the righteousness of God."

Of course, confronting a friend or family member's sin is even more challenging when you have been sinned against, and they either do not recognize their sin or they don't seem to care. It's easier to forgive sinners when they come to you humble and repentant! Even so, it's always wise to consider what "logs" may be present in my own eyes before addressing "specks" in others' eyes (Matthew 7:1–5).

PRAYER IS KEY

I also find the more faithful I am in praying for my children (or my friends or my counselees), the more attuned I am to where the Spirit may be convicting of "sin and righteousness and judgment" (John 16:8) in my own life as well as theirs. And the more convinced I am that it is not my responsibility (nor within my power) to change another person's heart, the more I can faithfully be an instrument in the Lord's hands. He is the one who ultimately brings sinners to repentance and empowers their obedience.

Consider how frequently and expansively Paul prays for the churches he had established. His letters certainly contain correction, instruction, and a call to holy living. But he demonstrates his dependence on the Spirit's work in these saints' lives through his prayers:

> I do not cease to give thanks for you, remembering you in my prayers, that the God of our Lord Jesus Christ, the Father of glory, may give you the Spirit of wisdom and of revelation in the knowledge of him, having the eyes of your hearts enlightened, that you may know what is the hope to which he has called you, what are the riches of his glorious inheritance in the saints, and what is the immeasurable greatness of his power toward us who believe, according to the working of his great might. (Ephesians 1:16–19)

For this reason I bow my knees before the Father, from whom every family in heaven and on earth is named, that according to the riches of his glory he may grant you to be strengthened with power through his Spirit in your inner being, so that Christ may dwell in your hearts through faith—that you, being rooted and grounded in love, may have strength to comprehend with all the saints what is the breadth and length and height and depth, and to know the love of Christ that surpasses knowledge, that you may be filled with all the fullness of God. (Ephesians 3:14–19)

And it is my prayer that your love may abound more and more, with knowledge and all discernment, so that you may approve what is excellent, and so be pure and blameless for the day of Christ, filled with the fruit of righteousness that comes through Jesus Christ, to the glory and praise of God. (Philippians 1:9–11)

And so, from the day we heard, we have not ceased to pray for you, asking that you may be filled with the knowledge of his will in all spiritual wisdom and understanding, so as to walk in a manner worthy of the Lord, fully pleasing to him: bearing fruit in every good work and increasing in the knowledge of God. (Colossians 1:9–10)

Prayer fuels humility and dependence in my own heart and unleashes the sanctifying power of the Spirit in the lives of brothers and sisters caught in sin.

LOOK BELOW THE SURFACE

I am also learning to expect that there is much under the surface I don't see at first glance. A sullen attitude rarely, if ever, means, "I got out of bed this morning and just decided to be as mean as I possibly could be." Rather, it could mean, "I got snubbed at school today and am feeling like an outsider," or "I couldn't get to sleep last night and now I feel physically horrible and I'm stressed about the midterm tomorrow," or "I can't get rid of this sadness and I don't why." I have found when I first seek an understanding of underlying heart issues and points of suffering—as well as potential physical, bodily contributors—my carefully probing concern often sparks repentance for the sullenness or disrespect, without me having to point it out explicitly. Similarly, in counseling ministry, if you're perplexed about why your counselees are persisting in particular patterns of sin, patiently dig deeper about possible desires, fears, and "treasures" that might be motivating them.

I'm a slow learner though in my own family. Too often I shoot first and ask questions later. So, if *I* sin in the midst of addressing *their* sin, then it's important to repent right then and there. As my daughter often says, "Can we start over?" What a picture of the gospel! Yes, we can always start over, because of Jesus. We both need that.

One final word here about addressing sin in our everyday relationships. Forbearance is not only an option; it's a command. Proverbs 19:11b (NIV) says, "it is to one's glory to overlook an offense." You don't get the sense that Jesus was "prickly" and easily offended like we sometimes are. We don't have to address a particular sin every time it occurs. You've heard the saying, "Pick your battles." Again, it's important to avoid the two extremes—going to war too quickly or never having the courage to fight the right battles. When we see significant and ongoing patterns of sin in others, we should prayerfully consider how God may be calling us to intervene.[1] Faithful friends, pastors, and counselors willingly engage in this rescue mission because they too need and have tasted the mercy of Jesus as they wrestle with sin in their own lives.

---

1. For more thoughts on this, see Alasdair Groves, "Nine Ways to Confront in Love: A Primer for the Timid," *The Journal of Biblical Counseling* 31, no. 1 (2017): 56–74.

Chapter 23

HOW WE LOVE SINNERS: COUNSELING EXAMPLES

How does this work in real life counseling situations? Let's start with Jared, a twenty-year-old man who grew up with an alcoholic, abusive father. The abuse was largely directed at his mother and his older brothers. He coped by withdrawing and turning inward or by people-pleasing—being just what people wanted or expected him to be—in order to minimize the chance of any conflict or relational strife. His mother is a believer, and Jared grew up going to church, although when I counseled him he was not exactly sure where he currently stood with God. In college, he began drinking and smoking marijuana regularly. He was an archeology major and on a recent dig project he had gravitated toward one of the team leaders—a married woman—who paid him a great deal of attention. This ultimately led to Jared having sex with her, which troubled him greatly and precipitated a depression that brought him to counseling.

Initially, Jared was very reluctant to frame things in biblical categories—he found talking about God very threatening and was more interested in foolproof behavioral steps that would keep him from having sex with married women. He enjoyed partying and drinking and wasn't ready to give up that lifestyle. In that context, he would occasionally hook up with a woman for a night. Sex with a married woman was clearly wrong in his eyes, but he viewed sex with single peers as morally ambiguous. These peer encounters didn't prick his conscience nearly as strongly as the affair, in which he saw himself as a "home-wrecker."

One continual sticking point was that he saw God as a cosmic killjoy and the Bible as a rule book that constrained his fun. Referencing Genesis 1:26–28 in passing, we spoke about God's original intent for humanity—to have the freedom to flourish as God's image bearers in a perfect creation under his wise and loving reign. Many years later at Mount Sinai, God gave commands to his people Israel, in part, to guide this newly redeemed and freed people into a way of living that was consistent with their status as God's covenant people. Rather than let us live with unrestrained instincts like the animals, his "rules" were actually meant to define the beautiful contours of life as God's unique image bearers. As J. Douma writes, "In the foreground of the law is not its strictness, but its concern to keep the one who has been liberated from falling back into slavery."[1] Jared admitted that his way of life, at the end of the day, was not flourishing. I saw a bit of softening in his heart.

WHAT IS REPENTANCE?

After a number of months of trying but failing to abstain from sex, he raised the issue, "What is repentance?" Sometimes in

1. J. Douma, *The Ten Commandments: Manual for the Christian Life*, trans. Nelson D. Kloosterman (Phillipsburg, NJ: P & R, 1996), 4.

ministry, God graciously pitches you a softball right down the middle! His conception of repentance was "I'm sorry, and I won't do it again." But now he was realizing that this approach did not supply him with the power to change.

I asked if we could read Psalm 51 together. My goal was to show that repentance is not only owning what *you* did, but owning who God is and what *he* does, which leads to restored relationship, freedom, joy, and service to others. We got out a white board and listed aspects of the passage that corresponded to "David owning his own stuff," and then listed aspects of the passage that corresponded to "David 'owning' who God is." I followed this by having him take the last fifteen minutes of our time together to journal an engagement with God. Specifically, I asked him, "In light of the patterns shown in this psalm, what does it look like for you to acknowledge and own your own sin and then couple that with who God is—what he has done on your behalf through Jesus?" As he wrote, he began to recognize his need for God to change and redirect his desires, which he was unable to do on his own.

WHO CAN MAKE US CLEAN?

About three weeks later Jared came in distraught. The married woman with whom he had the affair had contacted him after he had expressly asked her not to, at the end of the summer field work. He said, "It hit me hard. What I did came flooding back. *I did that!*" He felt guilt, fear, self-loathing, deep sadness, and a sense that he could never clean himself up. He would always be, "an adulterer." Who could cleanse him? I wanted him to see that only Jesus could provide the cleansing he needed. His efforts at self-discipline to cover his guilt were simply not working, nor could they ever. Where might you go in Scripture to pursue those goals? I turned to a passage that I had occasionally used in the past, Zechariah 3:1–5:

> Then he showed me Joshua the high priest standing before the angel of the Lord, and Satan standing at his right side to accuse him. And the Lord said to Satan, "The Lord rebuke you, Satan! The Lord who has chosen Jerusalem rebuke you! Is not this a brand plucked from the fire?" Now Joshua was standing before the angel, clothed with filthy garments. And the angel said to those who were standing before him, "Remove the filthy garments from him." And to him he said, "Behold, I have taken your iniquity away from you, and I will clothe you with pure vestments." And I said, "Let them put a clean turban on his head." So they put a clean turban on his head and clothed him with garments. And the angel of the Lord was standing by.

Zechariah was writing to the post-exilic community of God's people to call them to repentance (Zechariah 1:1–6) and to remind them in their discouragement that "the Lord will again comfort Zion and again choose Jerusalem" (1:17b). The passage I quoted above is followed by God's promise, "I will remove the iniquity of this land in a single day" (3:9b), which looks forward to the cleansing, redemptive work of Jesus Christ, "the Branch" (3:8).

What I wanted Jared to see was that he couldn't clean himself up, but God could. He removes our filthy, sinful clothing[2] and dresses us with pure garments, ultimately through

---

2. Joshua's "filthy" garments can be more precisely described as "garments soiled with excrement, which would automatically defile the wearer" according to a footnote in the *ESV Study Bible* (Wheaton, IL: Crossway, 2008), 1755. No amount of self-laundering could remove defilement before God.

the atoning work of Jesus Christ on the cross. In a staggering and mind-boggling exchange, he dons our tattered and soiled clothes and robes us with his spotless righteousness. All our best efforts cannot erase the mess. Jared was feeling the pinch of this reality in his own life. He needed what Luther called an "alien righteousness," a righteousness from outside himself through faith in Jesus Christ (Romans 3:21–24). We read the passage together, and he was clearly moved. For the first time since we had begun meeting, he allowed me to pray for him.

Notice that in our conversations, I didn't have to discern exactly where he stood with God. I didn't have to know for certain whether or not he was truly a saint to address his sin. He clearly viewed sin in behavioral and transactional categories (abstract rules) rather than in relational terms. Whether a child of God or not, the call was for him to forsake false loves and embrace the cleansing and forgiveness and the power to change through Jesus Christ.

I would love to say that as counseling moved forward, Jared yielded his life increasingly to Christ. But he didn't. We continued meeting for a few more months, but in the end, he decided that he was not ready to turn to Jesus. I appreciated his honesty, and we parted ways with him knowing that he could come back at any time.

MATT'S STORY: CAN I REALLY CHANGE?

Now, let's turn to Matt's story. Matt was a thirty-eight-year-old married man with three children who had a history of pornography use since his teen years. While the frequency of his use had decreased dramatically over the years since college, he still would view pornography every one to two months, despite the use of accountability software. "I can always find a loophole if I'm motivated," he admitted. He finds that one or two days each week have a higher level of sexual temptation. He has been honest with his wife when he has used pornography, and also with the two men he meets with weekly for Bible study and prayer. While Matt's wife is understandably hurt, she remains supportive of Matt and is glad for his honesty and for the growth he has experienced over time. Even so, she is weary from the spiritual and relational toll Matt's struggle is having on their marriage.

He came in wondering, "Can this really change? I know the Bible well. I even meet with the guys in my small group to help them with their struggle in this area. But I need help too." As we talked, we identified certain patterns associated with increased temptation. It often occurred when he felt exhausted, during or immediately after a period of intense work as the marketing director for an advertising agency. He regularly battled a fear of failure, despite receiving good performance reviews. He observed, "It seems like porn is one way to manage the stress and anxiety of my life." Here, heart issues included a fear of man, fear of failure, comfort-seeking, and control of unpleasant emotions, all bubbling beneath the surface of Matt's behaviors.

But he also struggled when he had slower times at work. In those situations, he recognized that boredom tempted him toward novelty seeking, including the challenge of finding a loophole. "When I don't have a pressing task to complete, that's when the internal churning and dissatisfaction begins." His bent toward novelty seeking showed up in his spiritual life as well. He found it difficult to consistently practice the basic spiritual disciplines. He would often switch from one devotional plan or aid to another without ever developing a rhythm. He said, "It's hard for me to live in the mundane. Ordinary life sometimes doesn't feel exciting enough." Here, heart issues of self-satisfaction and desire for immediate gratification/pleasure were evident.

It was helpful for Matt to see that there were multiple, well-worn pathways to his sexual sin, and that real change had to involve more than white-knuckling his unruly desires into submission. Gospel engagement at the heart level was key. As we continued to meet for several months, there were a number of things Matt and I worked on together.

One was to help him recognize his negative emotions (anxiety, fear of failure, etc.) and then talk about them honestly with the Lord rather than use the escape hatch of pornography. That was hard for him because engagement with God didn't necessarily automatically diminish his fears or his temptation. But he began to develop a pattern of perseverance in the midst of his temptation, "looking to Jesus, the founder and perfecter of our faith, who for the joy that was set before him endured the cross" (Hebrews 12:2a). Matt began to move from thinking, "How long can I go without giving in?" to "How can I look to Jesus and his abundant grace today?" He began to pray, "Help me to taste and see that you are good" (rewording Psalm 34:8) when he felt the siren call of "the fleeting pleasures of sin" (Hebrews 11:25b).

He began to gain a vision for "ordinary" daily kingdom living—loving his wife and family in simple words and deeds, and seeking to honor and serve Christ by his work (Galatians 1:10; 1 Corinthians 15:10). He was increasingly captured by Psalm 118:24, "This is the day that the LORD has made; let us rejoice and be glad in it." He stopped searching for a devotional "silver bullet" and simply sought to read a psalm and another short passage each day, reflecting the words of the passage back to God in prayer. Over time, he invited his wife to join him.

In addition, we talked about how to beef up his accountability software, locking down loopholes as much as possible, including his phone. He also began to text the men in his small group in real time when sexual temptation became stronger, and they, in turn, did the same.

During the months we met, Matt experienced a greater resolve to battle sexual temptation, and he viewed pornography less frequently. Most importantly, whether experiencing success or failure in the moment, he increasingly demonstrated Luther's observation that the Christian life "is not righteousness, but growth in righteousness, not health, but healing, not being, but becoming, not rest, but exercise. We are not yet what we shall be, but we are growing toward it. The process is not yet finished, but it is going on. This is not the end, but it is the road. All does not yet gleam in glory, but all is being purified."[3]

---

3. Martin Luther, "Defense and Explanation of All the Articles," in *Luther's Works,* ed. George W. Forell & Helmut T. Lehman, *vol. 32, Career of the Reformer II* (Minneapolis, MN: Fortress, 1958), 24.

Chapter 24

BARRIERS TO LOVING OTHERS AS SINNERS

As I reflected on a marriage counseling session that had just ended, I wondered if I could have done a better job loving these two sinners. No doubt, the husband's sin was front and center in our meetings—sloth, self-absorption, a biting sarcasm, and alcohol abuse. Her sins were "quieter"—perfectionism, control, and a self-righteous, judgmental spirit. Was I too hard on him? Was I too easy on her? I felt as though I had missed the mark with both of them.

Why do we struggle to love fellow sinners well? Why might we be hesitant to address sin in a person's life? Or we do address it, but in a harsh and unloving manner? Ask yourself if any of the following possible reasons may be true for you.

1. We forget that the saint and sufferer categories are always operative in the sinful person who knows Christ, and as a result, we only have eyes to see a person's sin. But do we remember, as

noted early in the book, that a believer's status as a saint is more primary and fundamental to his or her identity than is the category of sinner? As the subtitle of a book on identity I read years ago asks, *Christian, Do You Know Who You Are?*[1] We should never forget that our union with Jesus Christ is the grounding, motive, and power for our progressive sanctification. "We love because he first loved us" (1 John 4:19). Further, in view of others' experience of affliction, we should always keep in mind the pressure points of suffering that might "squeeze" their hearts, leading to the overflow of sin in thought, word, and deed. This realization fuels mercy and compassion even as we patiently address patterns of ongoing sin in the midst of their suffering.

2. We exhibit self-righteousness and a judgmental spirit in our approach, negating the impact of our words. As Christians, we should be the most humble of all people as we live out of the truth that God made us alive when we were dead and powerless in our sins. There is no room for self-congratulation (1 Corinthians 1:30–31). We should be humble, dependent, grateful receivers of Christ's mercy. Perhaps this is one reason why Alcoholics Anonymous is so helpful for many in coming alongside those caught in addictions, because you will hear statements such as, "I need the very same thing after forty years of sobriety that you need today after several weeks of binge drinking." Would others say that the description of the high priest in Hebrews 5:2 ("He can deal gently with the ignorant and wayward, since he himself is beset with weakness") characterizes us in our ministry?

3. We have a reactive rather than a proactive stance toward the sinner. When we experience sin in others' lives, particularly if it's directed toward us, we tend to react out of our own hurt and discomfort, rather than proactively considering the call to

---

1. David Needham, *Birthright: Christian, Do You Know Who You Are?* (Colorado Springs, CO: Multnomah, 2005).

love the other person well. Reacting in this way abandons the patient, others-centered engagement that characterizes God's way with sinners. No doubt this is difficult; we may need time to have God tend to our own wounds before we can constructively approach someone who has hurt us. Often, we face the temptation either to lash out or to remain silent and nurse a grudge against the other person. Neither approach is redemptive. We need the Spirit's enablement to "consider him [Jesus] who endured from sinners such hostility against himself, so that [we] may not grow weary or fainthearted" (Hebrews 12:3). When Jesus "was reviled, he did not revile in return; when he suffered, he did not threaten" (1 Peter 2:23a). We can only follow in the footsteps of Jesus as we continue "entrusting [ourselves] to him [God] who judges justly" (1 Peter 2:23b).

4. We struggle with fear of man and people-pleasing. If I want you to like me at all costs, it may cost too much to confront you on your sin, so I stay silent. The apostle Paul highlights the danger of this in Galatians 1:10–11, "For am I now seeking the approval of man, or of God? Or am I trying to please man? If I were still trying to please man, I would not be a servant of Christ." When I don't speak up out of fear, not only am I not loving the person well, I am not loving God well either. Variations on this theme include a fear of conflict or a fear that the person being confronted will end counseling or leave the church. It is true that drawing near to address sin in others' lives may produce conflict, strained relationships, and even further resistance that eventually culminates in church discipline. But we pray that God will use "a word in season" (Proverbs 15:23b) to help others experience the refreshment of repentance, so that together we might experience this reality: "Speaking the truth in love, we are to grow up in every way into him who is the head, into Christ" (Ephesians 4:15).

5. We are motivated by laziness, comfort, or the status quo. Sometimes it's just easier to ignore sin in another person. I know a husband and wife who each have significant patterns of ongoing sin. But they have an unspoken understanding that each will not interfere with the other. To call the other out on his or her sin would require change in themselves. Not to mention that the whole process of patiently walking with other sinners is often hard work. Do we care enough about a brother or sister caught in sin to move beyond our own discomfort and apathy?

6. Shame or guilt over our own sin makes us feel unworthy to address sin in others' lives. We may think, *Who am I to speak into this person's life when I'm a mess myself?* And yet, we are all people in process. Each of us, by God's grace, are seeking to keep in step with the Spirit (Galatians 5:16, 25). In fact, acutely feeling your own limitations and failures may give rise to a winsome humility and honesty as you speak with others. I often experienced this when my children were younger. Invariably, on the morning of a counseling day, some kind of parenting issue would arise in which I would become impatient, angry, or discouraged. Sometimes the problem could not even be resolved before I left for work, which often left me stewing in guilt and self-pity. By God's mercy (and providential irony), I usually had several people on my schedule that day who needed restoration from sin as I did. My own struggles made me more attuned to their guilt, shame, self-condemnation, and resistance to truth. Rather than disqualify me from ministering to fellow sinners, my own struggles led to compassion, judicious self-disclosure, and a hunger to mine the riches of God's word to help them. No doubt, I preached the gospel to myself on those days as much as I did to them!

THE PRIVILEGE OF TURNING OTHERS FROM SIN

To summarize Part 4 of this book, one of my favorite verses in Scripture (and one I pray for myself) is Malachi 2:6, which describes the ministry of Levi: "True instruction was in his mouth, and no wrong was found on his lips. He walked with me in peace and uprightness, and he turned many from iniquity." What an epitaph! To be an instrument in God's hands to lovingly and winsomely rescue brothers and sisters caught in sin is a high calling, and one given to all believers. May God give us grace to love fellow sinners in this way.

Part 5:
Remaining Balanced in Ministry

Chapter 25

A MINISTRY BALANCING ACT

Most often in personal ministry we encounter all three aspects of life as saint, sufferer, and sinner in one person at the same time. We constantly toggle between the saint, sufferer, and sinner aspects of people's lives depending on the needs of the hour (or minute). While I noted the general progression of saint → sufferer → sinner as we get to know someone initially, the most common situation in established relationships involves moving seamlessly between loving in each of the three modes. Most of the examples in the book have isolated one of the three for teaching and illustrative purposes, but now I want to pull all three aspects together in a single person.

SUSAN: A SAINT, SUFFERER, AND SINNER

Susan was a woman in her mid-thirties who struggled with crippling OCD that absorbed hours of her life each day. When I began meeting with her, she had pervasive anxiety that was diminished only when the dishes were clean, the carpet was vacuumed, and the tables and countertops were wiped down with bleach solution. She also was a highly competent biochemical researcher whose obsessive tendencies yielded well-planned and productive research. While she had a longstanding history of perfectionistic tendencies, what most haunted her when she looked into the mirror was seeing the woman she had been over a decade ago: a young college student, a scholar-athlete who had carefully and persistently lived up to the high academic and moral expectations of her parents. It was the perfect life—until she slept with her boyfriend, got pregnant, and had an abortion without telling him or anyone else. She vowed at that point never to lose control of her life again—and fifteen years later she had achieved that goal. Yet, her rule-based living and perceived control were fraying at the edges. She spent up to four hours per day ruminating, checking, and cleaning. She increasingly turned to alcohol at night to help her get to sleep. She longed for freedom.

She had grown up going to church, serving as a leader in her youth group, but since college she described her relationship with God as "distant." She spoke of her view of God this way: "He doesn't have time for me. He's upset with me. It's hard to believe he actually forgives and doesn't hold our sins against us." Not surprisingly, her view of herself corresponded to her view of God: "I'm a sinner worse than others. I'm alone and have to take care of myself. I have to do everything myself." When I asked her about the benefits she saw in relying on herself, she said, "It's safer. I can control things if I'm not relying on anyone else. If I make a mistake, it's mine. I can adjust and make changes going forward." She admitted at one point, "I think I would have made a good Pharisee!" She described her life as a pendulum that swung between anger at God ("I deserve your blessing for all these years of rule-keeping") and self-loathing ("I have failed miserably and am unworthy of your blessing"). She had avoided time alone with God over the years: "Will he reject me if his attention is drawn to me? If he sees me, he'll know my dark heart. Better just to keep my head down." At the same time, she had begun attending an evangelical church. Some new friends there suggested that she seek out biblical counseling. She said, "I know the path forward involves a return to Jesus, but I need a guide."

How do you understand Susan? How do you come alongside her as a friend, small group leader, pastor, or counselor? Where do you start? What's most important to make sense of her story? The oppressive expectations of her parents? Her sinful choices, past and present? Her current level of suffering? Her unbiblical views of God and self? Her success as a researcher? Her OCD diagnosis? The pervasive shame and guilt she still lives with? Something else? Or all of the above?

It might be easy to be overwhelmed with the details of Susan's life. You may think, *I don't know anything about OCD!* That may be true (and if so, it would be wise to involve a caregiver more seasoned in helping those with obsessions and compulsions) but you know more than you realize about this young woman who professes faith in Christ, particularly as you approach her as a saint, sufferer, and sinner. Let's see how care for her encompassed all three aspects over time.

SAINT

The very fact that Susan came in for counseling is evidence of the gracious work of God in her life. She wanted biblical perspective on her struggles, although there was still much that she didn't understand about herself and her problems. The Spirit was at work wooing her heart even before I had my first conversation with Susan. In addition to regularly attending church, she had recently committed herself to a small group. She was able to be vulnerable about her struggle with obsessions and compulsions and ask for prayer. These were aspects of her life worthy of celebration, which set the stage for addressing her struggles in more depth.

She started to spend time in Scripture, focusing on God's heart for his people. A distant, judgmental view of God coupled with a mistrust of his goodness gave way to a growing sense of God as her Abba Father (Galatians 4:6–7). She found especially helpful the Parable of the Prodigal Son (Luke 15:11–32). She saw herself in both the prodigal and the self-righteous older brother, and she was moved by the extravagant love of the father. She started to pray—more conversationally and more relationally. Her emotions, which Susan kept under tight control when we started to meet, were expressed with greater honesty and vulnerability before others and the Lord. Her life became less of a scorecard of successes and failures.

Throughout our meetings, I kept pointing out the good I saw, something she was hesitant to do. At one point, she told me she had shared honestly with her supervisor about her anxiety during a particular experiment. And she engaged with God in silent prayer throughout. "Turn to God; ask God for help" kept coming to her mind. We celebrated that she had taken a risk to be vulnerable before her supervisor and before God, rather than proceeding forward in tenuous self-sufficiency.

SUFFERER

Susan viewed herself primarily through the lens of her sinful choice in college. As we began meeting, she characterized herself primarily as a "selfish sinner," always on the cusp of doing something evil, restrained only by the rules that she lived by. "If

I'm not in control, I'll do something horrible to hurt others. I don't trust myself to make good decisions. If I follow the rules, it will be OK—nothing bad will happen."

Not only did Susan not think of herself as a saint, she downplayed her experiences as a sufferer. She said, "I stoically trudged through life weighed down by the knowledge that I had taken part in the giving and taking of life." She lived as if it were her duty to bear this heavy weight alone.

What should certainly strike us about Susan's story is the burden of her suffering for these last fifteen years. She was very high functioning in many ways, but she also lived in a prison of guilt, shame, fear, and suffocating rituals that took several hours a day. She walked through life with two massive weights tied to her ankles, trudging a lonely path.

What word of consolation could I provide? "The LORD was moved to pity by [her] groaning" (Judges 2:18b). "The LORD is near to the brokenhearted and saves the crushed in spirit" (Psalm 34:18). "He heals the brokenhearted and binds up their wounds" (Psalm 147:3). Jesus, inaugurating his ministry with the words of Isaiah 61, proclaimed:

> "The Spirit of the Lord is upon me,
>   because he has anointed me
>   to proclaim good news to the poor.
> He has sent me to proclaim liberty to the captives
>   and recovering of sight to the blind,
>   to set at liberty those who are oppressed,
> to proclaim the year of the Lord's favor." (Luke 4:18–19)

Over several months, Susan grew to embrace this proclamation of freedom. She increasingly called out to God for help in escaping her present misery.

With this growing freedom, she became increasingly willing to acknowledge and experience negative emotions such as sadness, guilt, shame, fear, and disappointment. A stoicism that had downplayed both her privilege as a daughter of God and her suffering gave way to a full-orbed engagement with God and others. The Psalms, which she had avoided because they put her face-to-face with honest, raw emotion, and threatened her tight control over her life, became a source of words to speak back to her faithful and compassionate God.

SINNER

Growth for Susan was not simply behavioral modification in which she spent less and less time doing her rituals. Such appropriate behavioral change needed to be linked to relationship with Jesus Christ. It was important for her to understand the heart behind her behavior. After several weeks of meeting together, listening to her story, and building relational trust, there were several heart-oriented themes we centered on.

Susan's vow, "I will never lose control again" was coming back to bite her. This vow was, in effect, a declaration of independence: "I can do this on my own and I will. I blew it once, but I won't blow it again." Her fear of losing control and ruining her life (again) worked out in a multiplicity of ways, including vigorous cleaning, triple checking her experimental data, and keeping a tight rein on her emotions. That was her safety, her broken cistern (Jeremiah 2:13).

Over time she also realized she was trying to do self-atonement by her compulsive behaviors. She recognized that she was trying to pay God back by being perfect at everything she did. She was committed to a works-based strategy of gaining favor with God, similar to the elder son in the Parable of the Prodigal

Son. She asked for and truly embraced the forgiveness of Christ, not only for her decisions in the past, but for her current ways of living apart from the grace and mercy of Christ. Interestingly, as this happened, we talked less and less about her OCD patterns; they quietly improved in keeping with the growing freedom she had before Christ. She had less need to obsessively control her life as she entrusted herself to a merciful Father, not a harsh taskmaster for whom she was doing endless penance.

She also recognized how much she hated to be weak and not in control. She admitted, "To receive God's mercy means I am weak and a failure. I have to trust him and relinquish control." This felt to her like starting to tumble down a big hill, "painful and uncontrollable." Giving up her rules and the perceived sense of control they brought felt like a loss of identity and safety for her and would mean a free-fall down the mountain into her worst-case scenarios of hurting herself and others. But as she marinated in the reality of God's great and loving heart for his people and how he works through weakness (1 Corinthians 1:18–2:5; 2 Corinthians 12:9), she was able to say, "I'm growing to trust that God really does have my back." This confidence prompted her to take the risk of not compulsively cleaning, which she did less of week by week, and it helped her turn from the escape alcohol had been for her.

Admitting the ways in which she sought life and security apart from Christ was critical for Susan's growth. And that is true for us as well. Freedom comes when the light of the gospel shines in the darkest places of our lives, even if our initial impulse is to run, cockroach-like, from the bright light. As I mentioned earlier, God does not reveal what he does not intend to heal, and Susan began to taste that blessed reality. She encountered a Savior whose "forgiving, redeeming, restoring touch reaches down into the darkest crevices of our souls, those places where we are most ashamed, most defeated."[1]

I hope you can see how these three categories of understanding are not discrete "compartments" of personal experience, nor do they engender separate and disconnected ministry responses from us. The experiences of being a saint, sufferer, and sinner are inseparable—like a rope with its strands all woven together into one whole. For example, confidence that God's banner over us is love (Song of Solomon 2:4) helps us endure suffering permitted by our loving Father *and* it compels us to live increasingly out of the privileges of our identity in thought, word, and deed. Scripture that brings consolation in suffering strengthens our trust that God is for us *and* motivates us to respond thankfully in obedience. Biblical clarity about our sinful behavior prompts repentance, a greater leaning on the work of Christ on our behalf, *and* relief from the misery of guilt, shame, and failure. This was true in Susan's life, and it is true in our own lives as well.

These three aspects of human experience are not meant to box you or anyone in. They are not meant to relativize or minimize the details of our life stories. Remember that they are anchor points for our experience. And that allows us to wade into deep complexities, tethered to the God who loves and moves toward his people as saints, sufferers, and sinners.

---

1. Dane Ortlund, *Gentle and Lowly: The Heart of Christ for Sinners and Sufferers* (Wheaton, IL: Crossway, 2020), 83.

Chapter 26

WHAT HAPPENS WHEN WE ARE IMBALANCED?

What happens when one aspect of our human experience becomes the *only* thing, functionally speaking, as we live our Christian lives? I am not speaking here of the times when God is at work in particular ways, which can bring one aspect of our lives front and center. For example, when, after hearing a sermon we have a fresh apprehension of our privileges as sons and daughters of God. Or when we are in a season of great suffering associated with a life-threatening illness. Or when God's Spirit has awakened a new awareness of and hatred for a particular pattern of sin in our lives. Rather, I'm talking about the situation when a person lives consistently as though only one aspect of the saint, sufferer, sinner triad really matters. In those cases, what should we be alert to in our own lives and in those we minister to?

OVEREMPHASIS ON SAINT

What happens when we overemphasize the "saint" aspect of our experience (i.e., *only* viewing ourselves through the lens of identity in Christ and the accomplished reality of our justification)?

First, we will tend to minimize wrongdoing, responsibility, and progressive growth in godliness. I once brought up, very carefully, to a person in my former church, something that had troubled me about his behavior toward me. His response caught me by surprise: "Don't you put me under the law! I'm a child of the King!" For this person, owning his responsibility and pursuing obedience were somehow disconnected from being a son or daughter of King Jesus. What mattered to him was his positional standing in Christ; that reality overshadowed any of the moral imperatives of Scripture, at least practically speaking.

But we never see that disconnect in the Bible. We see a "both/and" in Scripture through the pairing of indicative and imperative, but this brother in Christ lived life as if it were an "either/or." What he wanted, in effect, was a Christianized version of "unconditional positive regard," which resulted in him being prickly and unapproachable in relationships if anyone even hinted at wrongdoing. His functional theology had no place for verses like, "as he who called you is holy, you also be holy in all your conduct" (1 Peter 1:15). Ironically, his posture robbed him of the opportunity to taste the mercy of Jesus in the midst of confession of sin.

Second, even if we take sin seriously, the main emphasis in progressive sanctification may be reduced to "just remember your justification" as opposed to taking concrete and habitual steps of obedience that form us as disciples of Christ.[1] Meditating on our position in Christ does nourish and deepen our faith, but we also

---

1. See David Powlison, *How Does Sanctification Work?* (Wheaton, IL: Crossway, 2017), 45–55.

grow by living out the commands and prohibitions of Scripture. Consider the active response of the Corinthians to Paul's challenge about the immorality in their fellowship: earnestness, godly grief, eagerness to clear themselves, indignation, fear, longing, zeal, and taking appropriate disciplinary steps (2 Corinthians 7:10–12).

Third, we project a breezy cheerfulness that fails to connect with the brokenness and suffering in other people's lives. No doubt, we should exult in the amazing reality that God has called, justified, and adopted us. No doubt, joy should be characteristic of our lives as believers (Psalm 16:11; Isaiah 61:10; Romans 5:11; 1 Peter 1:8). We are his children and he is accomplishing his purposes in our lives (1 Corinthians 1:8; Philippians 1:6). But living as a saint isn't an abstract, other-worldly, overly-cognitive affair, but a boots-on-the-ground experience of life in a world that has not been fully rescued from its suffering and sin. Groaning over what fundamentally remains broken is a characteristic posture of saints who already possess the Spirit of adoption as children (Romans 8:15–16, 23; 2 Corinthians 5:4–5).

In truth, more frequently our temptation is not to exaggerate this foundational aspect of our experience, but to minimize it or just give a "yeah, I know that." I recognize that's my tendency. But I would argue that without keeping before us the fundamental identity shift that has occurred for those in Christ Jesus, we cannot rightly address the experiences of suffering and sin that mark our lives this side of glory. Without an identity grounded in Jesus Christ, I will view myself primarily as either a victim or as a villain. But if I understand myself as a saint who suffers and a saint who sins, it reorients me. I begin to see, perhaps dimly at first, that my suffering puts me in the closest possible relationship with my Suffering King. And I recognize my sin as an aberration, a temporary deviation from my true identity, and I increasingly long to live as I was designed to live.

OVEREMPHASIS ON SUFFERER

What happens when we overemphasize the "sufferer" aspect of our lives? When we have eyes to see *only* the hardships of life?

First, we view ourselves principally as victims. The only thing that is important in our story is how others have wronged us or the difficulties that we face. Complaining about and to others, rather than lamenting to God characterizes our life. Our hardship is the sun around which our life orbits.

No doubt, those who have been sinned against have indeed been victimized. All the more so if the traumas are severe. We saw earlier in the book God's heart for the oppressed and persecuted. That's why God gives words such as those we find in Psalm 10 to people who are being (or have been) victimized, to pray back to him:

> But you do see, for you note mischief and vexation,
>> that you may take it into your hands;
> to you the helpless commits himself;
>> you have been the helper of the fatherless.
> Break the arm of the wicked and evildoer;
>> call his wickedness to account till you find none.
> (10:14–15)

> O Lord, you hear the desire of the afflicted;
>> you will strengthen their heart; you will incline your ear
> to do justice to the fatherless and the oppressed,
>> so that man who is of the earth may strike terror no
> more. (10:17–18)

It is wise and good for victims to work through their pain, before God and others. That process may indeed be lifelong for some forms of suffering. But over time, is that journey leading toward a destination that increasingly frees the person from the shackles of a victim identity? Are people moving toward God more consistently, rather than away from him, even if they stumble in a given moment? A personal narrative focused primarily on the hardships of life is centripetal (spiraling inward), rather than centrifugal (spiraling outward). By contrast, those who have experienced deep hurt and trial *and* who have known the consolation of God and others, are particularly equipped to minister comfort to other hurting saints.

Second, we become focused on strategies for escaping suffering because we believe the greatest good is to eradicate suffering in our lives. On the one hand, as we saw earlier in the book, this mind-set reveals an important truth—all history is moving toward the extinction of suffering under the reign of Jesus Christ. But on the other hand, do we also embrace the reality that suffering now in Christ confirms our identity as children of God? I referenced this passage earlier, but it's important to highlight it again: "The Spirit himself bears witness with our spirit that we are children of God, and if children, then heirs—heirs of God and fellow heirs with Christ, provided we suffer with him in order that we may also be glorified with him" (Romans 8:16–17). This is a hard truth to hear, understand, and embrace. As the man in Mark 9:24 exclaimed to Jesus, I too say, "I believe; help my unbelief!"

Without this Christ-centered perspective on suffering, we miss the solidarity we have with Jesus as we suffer. We miss God's refining and transforming work in the midst of our hardships. If we see suffering as only a horrible, meaningless end in itself, we miss that God is treating us as beloved children (Hebrews 5:5–11). We miss that suffering restrains sin in our lives (Psalm 119:67; 2 Corinthians 12:7). We miss redemption-in-progress amidst the darkness in our own lives, in others' lives, and in the world. And so, a pervasive dread and hopelessness marks our days. Or a detached stoicism as we wait for our earthly prison sentence to end. No, I want to be able to affirm, "Suffering is not an embarrassment to the Christian faith. It is the thread with which Christ's name is stitched into our lives."[2]

Third, we are likely to minimize wrongdoing and responsibility in our own life. We will underplay our agency as victimizers and sinners. I am counseling a man who neglected and abused his children when they were younger, in the midst of mental health and addiction challenges that he attributes to his own abusive upbringing. Although he laments the estrangement in his relationship with his (now) adult children, and although he continues to experience shame and guilt over his mistreatment of them, he complains most often about the way his children don't seem to get how hard his life was as a child and as a young parent. Needless to say, his children are not very amenable to reconciliation because he views himself mainly as a victim, rather than as someone who also inflicted grievous harm on others.

Fourth, we will live without hope. We will hear only the first part of Jesus's statement to his worried disciples: "In the world you will have tribulation," but not the second: "But take heart; I have overcome the world" (John 16:33). Without having the perspective that God has begun the work of making all things new in Christ Jesus (2 Corinthians 5:17; Revelation 21:5), the suffering in our lives and in the lives of those we love will swallow us up. In the "already" and "not yet" reality of Jesus's kingdom (Hebrews 2:8–10), the "not yet" will dominate our lives. The promise of a new heavens and earth will seem distant and irrelevant to our lives today, which are marked with so much sorrow and difficulty.

---

2. Rebecca McLaughlin, *Confronting Christianity: 12 Hard Questions for the World's Largest Religion* (Wheaton, IL: Crossway, 2019), 205.

OVEREMPHASIS ON SINNER

What happens when we overemphasize the "sinner" aspect of our experience as Christians?

First, we focus only on what needs to change rather than celebrating the good that God has already accomplished in our and others' lives. We live as spiritual Scrooges with an internal "Bah, humbug!" when there is good reason for encouragement. Or if we acknowledge the encouragement, it is a solitary and effervescent blip in a sea of negativity and self-critique. We squirm out from under God's benediction as if "well done, good and faithful servant" (Matthew 25:21, 23) is radioactive to our souls rather than the balm we desperately need. Ultimately, we are critical and condemning of ourselves—and others.

Second, it's easy to transfer that negativity onto our view of God. If all that really matters is ridding ourselves of sin, and we regularly fail at it (which we will) it's easy to envision God as a harsh taskmaster whose countenance toward us is a perpetual frown. We will imagine him always viewing us through a film of displeasure. We will hear him say, "Get your act together" or "Shouldn't you be over this by now?" more than "If you confess your sins, [I am] faithful and just to forgive [your] sins and to cleanse [you] from all unrighteousness" (1 John 1:9). We won't hear, "Come to me, all who labor and are heavy laden, and I will give you rest. Take my yoke upon you, and learn from me, for I am gentle and lowly in heart, and you will find rest for your souls. For my yoke is easy, and my burden is light" (Matthew 11:28–30). Instead, we will experience him adding rocks to our backpack as we dutifully trudge on.

Third, a legal rather than a relational ethos characterizes our lives. Laws, rules, and commands are at the forefront of our minds rather than our union with Christ and the gift of living under his benediction. It becomes easy to fall into a works and performance mentality, even if our confessional theology would never permit us to say that we are saved by works and not by grace. For many years in my Christian life, I articulated that I was saved by grace, but *lived* as if I were saved by the sweat of my brow on a treadmill of works, burdened by guilt and shame in the wake of failure.

Fourth, an overemphasis on sin can lead to focusing on concrete rules and guidelines that end up missing the heart, as happened with the Pharisees. This is why we can "do the right thing" and still be insufferable to others!

Fifth, our reading of Scripture becomes truncated. We miss the beauty and the glory of the outworking story of God's redemption in Scripture. It becomes wallpaper that fades behind the question, "What am I supposed to do?" Of course, reading Scripture *should* prompt us to ask, "Lord, how ought your words impact my life?" But if we have eyes only for commandments, sin, and personal responsibility as we read Scripture, we will rush to action rather than lingering on and enjoying what God says about himself, which is foundational for grace-empowered, grateful obedience. Remember, Scripture is first and foremost a story about the triune God who inaugurates a rescue mission for his wayward image bearers and his broken creation.

Sixth, there is no real hope for redemption or change. We would not *say* this of course! But an exclusive focus on how you or others are missing the mark leads to a "never enough" mentality. Our identity never shifts from sinner to saint. We *are* our sins. This is how Javert viewed Jean Valjean in *Les Misérables*—always and only as prisoner 24601, a parolee who had served nineteen years for stealing bread and then trying to escape from prison.[3]

---

3. See Victor Hugo, *Les Misérables* (New York: Penguin Classics, 1982).

It is difficult to get the balance right. We should never be satisfied and mistakenly think that we've "arrived" in terms of our growth in holiness. We must take seriously the multiple admonitions in Scripture to pursue godliness, such as: "Strive for peace with everyone, and for the holiness without which no one will see the Lord" (Hebrews 12:14), or "For God has not called us for impurity, but in holiness" (1 Thessalonians 4:7). But as we saw earlier in the book, God ultimately grounds the call to obedience in the work of salvation he has already accomplished in Jesus Christ, which is then applied in the renewing of our hearts. Second Corinthians 6:18–7:1 reminds us of this relationship: "'and I will be a father to you, and you shall be sons and daughters to me, says the Lord Almighty.' Since we have these promises, beloved, let us cleanse ourselves from every defilement of body and spirit, bringing holiness to completion in the fear of God." We are beloved sons and daughters—saints! That motivates us to wage war against sin in our lives.

BALANCING WELL

Keeping these three categories in view guards us from absolutizing any one aspect of our lives, which leads to oversimplification and distortion. And they keep us from being imbalanced as we minister to others. David Powlison once said, "True wisdom is not marked by a simple accumulation of knowledge, but by a growing ability to hold together complementary biblical truths without allowing any one of them to be eclipsed."[4] Ministering wisely means that we hold all three aspects of human experience together even if at a given point in time, we focus on one because that is most needful for the person in front of us.

---

4. David Powlison, personal conversation. (An abbreviated version of this idea is found in *How Does Sanctification Work?*, 67.)

Chapter 27

WHERE THERE IS NO SUFFERING OR SIN

Throughout this book I have been making the case that our experience as fallen and redeemed human beings maps onto the biblical categories of saint, sufferer, and sinner. But that won't always be the case. One day we will experience full redemption. Who we truly are now as saints in Christ will come to mind-boggling fruition (1 Corinthians 2:9). Present groaning will turn to glory (Romans 8:18–23). On that day, suffering, death, and sin will no longer permeate and stain the fabric of our day-to-day lives. We will worship God in glorious freedom as his sons and daughters before his throne, in the new heavens and earth, unencumbered by hardship, pain, tears, the world, the flesh, and the devil. We will be saints who no longer suffer, saints who no longer sin. This is our destiny as believers. This is the destiny we invite non-believers to embrace.

FOCUSING ON OUR MAGNIFICENT FUTURE

Clearly, we do not simply mark time while we await that day. Being shaped and refined in the crucible of suffering *now* readies us for that day. Battling sin and growing in Christlikeness *now* readies us for that day. Like people-moving sidewalks in airports, redemptive history is taking us somewhere, and we want to keep our eyes focused on the destination ahead and keep our steps aligned with the movement of the Spirit.

But God knows we become weary. Suffering threatens to swallow up joy and hope. In the bruising battle against remaining sin, we too often wave the white flag of surrender. This is true for those we love and minister to as well. Together we cry out with the apostle Paul, "Who will deliver me from this body of death?" (Romans 7:24b). Together we rejoice at his reply and yearn for its consummation: "Thanks be to God through Jesus Christ our Lord!" (Romans 7:25).

In our journey together, I have highlighted how Jesus has called us to himself as saints and is at work through his Spirit, delivering us from suffering and sin. But as you near the end of your reading, I want you to linger on the picture God paints of this deliverance as it comes to its completion. Let these amazing visions of everlasting life motivate you to press forward in your own walk with Christ and encourage you as you minister to others:

> Then I saw a new heaven and a new earth, for the first heaven and the first earth had passed away, and the sea was no more. And I saw the holy city, new Jerusalem, coming down out of heaven from God, prepared as a bride adorned for her husband. And I heard

a loud voice from the throne saying, "Behold, the dwelling place of God is with man. He will dwell with them, and they will be his people, and God himself will be with them as their God. He will wipe away every tear from their eyes, and death shall be no more, neither shall there be mourning, nor crying, nor pain anymore, for the former things have passed away." (Revelation 21:1–4)

Then the angel showed me the river of the water of life, bright as crystal, flowing from the throne of God and of the Lamb through the middle of the street of the city; also, on either side of the river, the tree of life with its twelve kinds of fruit, yielding its fruit each month. The leaves of the tree were for the healing of the nations. No longer will there be anything accursed, but the throne of God and of the Lamb will be in it, and his servants will worship him. They will see his face, and his name will be on their foreheads. And night will be no more. They will need no light of lamp or sun, for the Lord God will be their light, and they will reign forever and ever. (Revelation 22:1–5)

The writer of Hebrews highlights that Jesus, "for the joy that was set before him endured the cross, despising the shame" (Hebrews 12:2b). May we also, for the certain joys set before us in these passages, press forward in Christ-centered hope as saints who will one day cast off for eternity both suffering and sin. "For all the promises of God find their Yes in him. That is why it is through him that we utter our Amen to God for his glory" (2 Corinthians 1:20). Amen and Amen!

LOVE IN KEEPING WITH OUR GLORIOUS DESTINY

The ways we love fellow believers should be in keeping with this glorious destiny. We love well when we affirm and encourage a person's identity in Christ, pointing out where we see the Spirit at work. We love well when we bring consolation, hope, and help in the midst of a friend's affliction. We love well when we bring admonition to highlight and correct sin.

Remembering the categories of saint, sufferer, and sinner doesn't give us specific words to say (or not to say) to a specific person at a particular time. Wise love doesn't come packaged as a formula. But keeping in mind these biblical facets of our human experience provides a framework for understanding ourselves and our fellow brothers and sisters in Christ. Coupled with the Spirit's wisdom in a given ministry moment, we have more than enough guidance to shape our love to them.

One writer observed that a friend is someone who helps you re-narrate your life in light of the good news of Jesus Christ.[1] That is, a friend is someone who wisely helps you reinterpret your experiences according to the life-giving contours of the gospel. May God help us grow in being this kind of person to one another—true friends and fellow saints, sufferers, and sinners.

---

1. Stephen E. Fowl, *Philippians, The Two Horizons New Testament Commentary* (Grand Rapids, MI: Eerdmans, 2005), 208, 220–26.

ACKNOWLEDGMENTS

Every book is a team effort. Many conversations and ministry opportunities over the years have contributed to the development of this material and I am deeply grateful for all of them, even if I am not able to mention each one here.

Thanks to Mark and Karen Teears of New Growth Press for publishing my first book over a decade ago: *CrossTalk: Where Life & Scripture Meet*, in which I first introduced the saint, sufferer, and sinner triad.

In April 2016, I had the privilege of speaking at the Biblical Counselling UK (BCUK) residential conference, where I taught on the use of Scripture in ministering to saints, sufferers, and sinners. Many thanks to Steve Midgley, Executive Director of BCUK, and the BCUK Executive Committee for inviting me, and for the gracious hospitality of Steve and his wife, Beth, at their Cambridge home. (Little did I know that "punting" involved something other than kicking an American football!)

I was able to develop and hone these concepts in two *Journal of Biblical Counseling* articles: "Loving Others as Saints, Sufferers, and Sinners (Part 1)" *Journal of Biblical Counseling* 32, no. 1 (2018): 33–47 and "Loving Others as Saints, Sufferers, and Sinners (Part 2)" *Journal of Biblical Counseling* 32, no. 2 (2018): 40–65. I want to thank *JBC* editors Kim Monroe and Lauren Whitman for their biblical wisdom, patience, and editorial skill, which have borne much fruit over the years, including a much smoother on-ramp for the writing of this book.

I am profoundly thankful for the many hours of conversations with friends, family, and counselees, whose stories breathe life and authenticity to this book. While I have changed identifying details of actual counseling cases or constructed case composites, they represent accurately the people whom I have had the privilege of walking beside as a spiritual friend and pastoral counselor.

I never tire of working alongside fellow CCEF faculty members Alasdair Groves, Jayne Clark, Ed Welch, Julie Lowe, Cecelia Bernhardt, Todd Stryd, and Aaron Sironi. They are a joy and the aroma of Christ to me. So was the late David Powlison, whom I dearly miss. I am grateful also to co-labor with the broader CCEF staff who are like family to me. I also wish to thank the anonymous donor whose generous gift to CCEF funded my partial writing sabbatical during Fall 2019, which resulted in significant progress on the manuscript.

Thanks to the entire team at New Growth Press for all their labors to bring this book to fruition—you are unsung publishing heroes on whose shoulders authors stand! I am indebted to my editor Barbara Juliani, who patiently—there's that word again—and enthusiastically took up the task of working with me in the midst of her broader responsibilities as Vice President and Editorial Director at New Growth Press.

This resource is far better because of her editorial skills and years of ministry experience.

My wife, Jody, has seen my life as a saint, sufferer, and sinner more closely than any other person on earth. And amazingly, she still wants to be married to me! She is a model of Christlikeness in all ways. Her genuine love for others, her tender heart of mercy, her dogged, Spirit-dependent perseverance in the midst of many hardships, and her zeal for honoring her Savior, spur on my own faith.

Finally, I am profoundly thankful for my children, Lydia and Luke, who are beginning to spread their wings as young adults. They regularly amaze me with their gifts and grit. This book is dedicated to them.

SCRIPTURE INDEX

8:34	10	3:23	10, 119
11:33–35	91	3:23–24	7
14:6	50	5:3b–4	81
14:16	114	5:5	114
14:16–18	76	5:6–11	119
14:16, 25–26	29	5:8	138
14:18, 27b	84	5:11	176
15:5	125	5:12–21	13
16:7	115	6:1–7:6	29
16:8	148	6:2	10
16:33	79, 179	6:11	26
		6:12–13	123
		6:17	9
ACTS		7:21	7
2:33	115	7:24	121, 184
3:11–26	24	7:25	121, 184
7	24	8:3–4	7, 17
10:38	7, 68	8:14–15	9
13	24	8:15	14, 22
17:22–28	49	8:15–16	176
		8:15–17	22
		8:16–17	70, 178
ROMANS		8:16–25	70
1:1–4	14	8:18–23	183
1:1–15	31	8:22–23	67
1:4	13	8:23	176
1:18–32	49	8:26	91
1:25	134	11	20
2:4	10, 145	12:10	3
3:10–12	119	15:14	3
3:21–24	156		